THE BASICS OF INFORMATION WORK

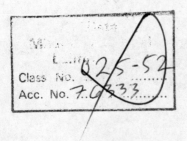

THE BASICS OF INFORMATION WORK

ALLAN BUNCH

CLIVE BINGLEY LONDON

Copyright © Allan Bunch 1984. Published by Clive Bingley Limited, 7 Ridgmount Street, London WC1E 7AE, and printed in England by Redwood Burn Limited, Trowbridge, Wiltshire. All rights reserved. No part of this publication may be photocopied, recorded or otherwise reproduced, stored in a retrieval system or transmitted in any form or by any electronic or mechanical means without the prior permission of the copyright holder and publisher.

First published 1984

British Library Cataloguing in Publication Data

Bunch, Allan
    The basics of information work.
    1. Information services
    I. Title
    025.5'2   Z674.4

    ISBN 0 85157 376 2

Typeset by Allset in 11 on 12 point Baskerville
1 2 3 4 5 88 87 86 85 84

Contents

Introduction

This book is one of a series intended to provide a basic introduction to the subject. It is aimed at both the younger professional librarian who is interested in extending the scope of an existing reference service to meet special needs in the community and those who are called upon to set up or operate an information service but have no training in librarianship or experience of information handling skills. In trying to cater for these two groups, the book is in great danger of not satisfying either by being too elementary or too complicated. I have tried to overcome this by including both cheap and simple solutions as well as more complicated and expensive ones.

The text is based largely on my own experience of setting up community information services in Peterborough and many of the examples are drawn from local material. This is not to imply that these are the only or the best examples; indeed there are many such services in existence doing excellent work. It was simply a matter of convenience to use material at hand rather than spend time searching for it.

My task was made very much easier by being able to refer to an excellent report not widely available in this country, namely *Establishing a local community information service* by Anne L Keehan and Catherine Riatti (Library Board of Western Australia, 1982, 2vols) and I duly acknowledge my indebtedness to it for providing me with a framework from which to work. I would also like to thank Nick Moore for his invaluable advice and encouragement, Elaine Kempson, Grainne Morby (Community Information Project), Pam Wright (Lambeth Libraries) and everyone else who provided me with information or lent material.

Chapter One

Who needs an information service?

Many organizations, from national campaigning bodies to local tenants' groups, from time to time feel the need to set up an information service to meet the requirements of either their own staff or membership; the general public as a whole or belonging to a defined geographical area; sections of the public with particular needs, such as disabled or elderly people, managers of small businesses, tourists, or the 'disadvantaged'; or workers and public associated with a particular purpose that usually has a finite time-scale, eg a redevelopment scheme or anti-dampness campaign.

It may sound obvious to state that, before setting up an information service, you should ask yourself, first of all, some very basic questions — like those a journalist asks when writing a story — who?, what?, when?, where?, why?, and how?, but not necessarily in that order! Surprisingly, there are many instances where these questions have not been asked and services have been set up which were either not wanted, the wrong type of service to meet users' needs, a duplication of already existing services, too ambitious for available staffing or resources, or lacking in commitment from the organizations's management or staff.

The moral is that careful thought and preparation at the outset can save a lot of wasted effort and be the sound foundation on which to build a successful service. It is always better to start modestly and grow, than to be too ambitious and have to retract or fail completely. This book tries to follow the same principle in the way its information is presented, moving from simple methods to the more sophisticated. But first of all, let us consider those basic questions.

Why set up an information service?

Everybody has information needs but not everybody is equally capable of satisfying those needs.[1] This is increasingly so in what has been termed our 'information society', with its complexity and rapidly accelerating rate of political, social and economic change. Therefore, a good reason for setting up an information service may well be to make it easier for individuals or groups of people who do not have their own adequate information networks to gain access to information that can be of benefit to them.

Some needs that warrant particular attention are:

(a) *inner city areas* where multiple deprivation exists — bad housing, high unemployment, inadequate schools — or where there is a greater proportion of ethnic minorities and transient populations.

(b) *housing estates* which lack basic social and other amenities — meeting places, recreational space, shops — where transport is inadequate or expensive, housing is bad and repairs deficient, vandalism rife.

(c) *rural areas* where facilities — shops, post offices, doctors, clergy, local government services, transport — are fast disappearing.

(d) *groups with special needs* — low income families, elderly and disabled people, ethnic minorities, tourists, young people, managers of small businesses, community and social workers, local government officials and elected members.

It is not a good idea to set up an information service because other agencies are doing so and you do not want to be left out. There has to be substantial evidence of a need for such a service in the local community or amongst your clientele to justify provision. Which leads to the next question:

Who needs an information service?

Rarely will the need for an information service be readily apparent or clearly voiced by your clientele, more often than not that need will have to be identified and assessed. There are several ways of finding out who needs an information service, ranging from the simple to the sophisticated. Here are a few methods you may care to consider:

(a) *Talk* to the 'gate-keepers' in your community — these are the people who, because of the nature of their work, their knowledge, approachability or status, others go to for information and advice. A typical list of 'gate-keepers' will include community workers, health visitors, councillors, social workers, trade union stewards, youth leaders, headteachers, Women's Institute secretaries. A word of caution. You should not rely on the views of these people alone, they may well be biased or blinkered. When a research worker, carrying out a project to identify the information needs of a remote rural area of Northumberland,[2] asked local community leaders for their views, the replies indicated that there were no information needs. And yet a subsequent sample survey of homes revealed that this was very far from the truth. So, it is important to check out the views of community leaders or 'gate-keepers' with those of your potential clientele and by using some of the other methods below.

(b) *Contact* groups and attend meetings. Find out if there are any groups which represent the people you wish to serve, as they will most likely be aware of the needs of their members or the community. Particularly useful are 'umbrella' groups like Councils for Voluntary Service (CVSs), Rural Community Councils (RCCs), Councils for the Disabled, Trades Councils, Chambers of Trade and Commerce, Community Associations, and Associations of Hoteliers (for tourist information needs). Look out also for less formal groups such as luncheon clubs for community workers, youth leaders or advice workers. Attending meetings of groups like these will give you a feel for the kind of problems that arise and where provision is lacking. For example, arising out of a series of training meetings on welfare rights which I attended, came the need for an information bulletin to keep advice workers up to date with changes in regulations and informed on local issues. Such meetings might also be a useful forum to discuss a proposed information service.

If your 'community' is a closed one, such as the staff of a particular organization, then it is important for you as information officer or librarian to have the right to sit in on committee meetings. In this way you will more quickly become familiar with the concerns of the organization and so identify what its information needs are likely to be and how to meet them. However, you may need to convince committee members of the desirability of this and one of the best ways is is prove your worth by providing them with some information, possibly on subjects under discussion in the committee.

(c) *Arrange an informal meeting* of representatives of groups in your community and other interested or useful people at which you can discuss your ideas for an information service and progress further if necessary. Out of this meeting might well be set up a steering committee or working group which could canvass wider opinion, either informally, by calling an open meeting, or by conducting a survey of the community. Such a group might also prepare a feasibility study.

(d) *Call an open meeting* at which your 'community' can hear about the proposals and make comments. If the meeting is not being called by the kind of steering committee suggested above, in some circumstances where, for example, your organization, rightly or wrongly, is regarded by the community as representing one particular viewpoint, it may be helpful for the meeting to be called under the auspices of a more 'neutral' body.

Wide publicity for the meeting is essential, using whatever means are available — word of mouth, posters, leaflets, local press, periodicals, newsletters, etc. Try to get the publicity into those areas where large numbers of your 'community' are likely to see it. Any publicity should give details of what the meeting is about, when and where it is being held and at what time.

Choose a date and venue that is convenient to most of the people you want to reach, taking care to avoid any other events or activities that are likely to prove a counter attraction. It is wise to give some thought to the ambience of the venue for, in some cases, an imposing room or 'official' building may inhibit attendance or discussion. Avoid obvious blunders like holding a meeting on an upper-floor without wheelchair access if you are proposing an information service for the disabled! Refreshments, if only a cup of coffee, add a touch of informality and encourage discussion. Put yourself in the place of someone who might attend the meeting and ask what would attract *you*.

Make careful preparations before the meeting takes place, including a plan of how you would like the meeting to be structured, so that discussion does not waffle on aimlessly and yet is flexible enough to encourage responses from the audience. Graphic displays, audio-visual presentations and speakers from similar projects elsewhere can add another dimension and help to get across your ideas.

Some further tips about the meeting:

— you will need someone, preferably a respected figure in your community, to open the meeting, explain what it is all about, and chair the proceedings

— keep items as brief as possible; people soon get bored with lengthy speeches

— encourage questions and contributions from the floor even to the extent of 'planting' a few to break the ice

— end the meeting before people get restive or discussion degenerates into irrelevancies

— make it clear what the next step is going to be. If there is support for your ideas then you may want to form a committee from those present. Alternatively, this step may still be premature, in which case arrange a further meeting of interested parties. Take note of the names and addresses of those expressing an interest so that you can keep them informed of future meetings and developments.

For more advice on planning meetings, there is a useful book called *A guide to effective meetings* by M Pemberton (Industrial Society, Peter Runge House, 3 Carlton House Terrace, London SW1Y 5DG, 1983, £1.95).

So, by the end of the open meeting, you should have some measure of support or interest from the community in your proposed information service. It is important that the community or users of the proposed service are given an opportunity to participate both in its planning and running, so that it matches their needs and is responsive to changing circumstances. If there is no support, it would be unwise to go ahead, certainly in the form that was proposed.

(e) *Conduct a survey* of potential users to establish their information needs. This can be done instead of or additional to holding an open meeting. It is essential from the start that you have a clear idea of what you want to get out of the survey and at whom it is aimed, for this will determine the kind of questions you will want to ask and the form in which you present them. It is a good principle always to try to

```
SOUTH MOLTON LIBRARY: COMMUNITY INFORMATION PROJECT          "20 QUESTIONS"
Please fill in the answers requested, or delete the words which do not apply.  (If you have
already received and completed one of these, please pass it to a friend).
```

1.	On what subjects have you needed information, advice or help in the past year? Examples: education, housing, tax, holidays.	....
2.	To which organisations or people have you turned for such help? Examples: neighbour, solicitor, councillor, Citizens' Advice Bureau, Volunteer Bureau	....
3.	How often do you use South Molton Library?	Frequently/occasionally/never
4.	Do you use any other library in the area? Yes/no	If so which? ....
5.	How often do you use the mobile library service based on South Molton?	Frequently/occasionally/never
6.	Do you use another mobile or other service? Yes/no Example: school library. How often?	If so which? .... Frequently/occasionally/never
7.	Do you have access to a telephone? Yes/no	If so which? Own 'phone/ neighbour's 'phone/public call box or payphone
8.	Do you listen to Morning Sou' West (BBC radio)?	Yes/no
9.	Do you have a television?	Yes/no
10.	Do you normally do your weekly shopping in South Molton?	Yes/no
11.	If not, which town do you visit?	....
12.	Do you drive or have access to a vehicle?	Yes/no
13.	If not, how far are you from the nearest 'bus stop served by a weekly or more frequent service to South Molton?	....
14.	Which local newspapers and magazines do you read? (Include parish newsletters and magazines)	....
15.	How long have you lived in the South Molton area?	....
16.	If you are not a "native" of the area, where did you live before moving here?	....
17.	How far do you live from the centre of South Molton?	....
18.	Which of the following age groups are you in? (Male) (Please put a tick in the appropriate box) (Female)	0-16☐ 17-39☐ 40-64☐ 65+☐ 0-16☐ 17-39☐ 40-59☐ 60+☐

```
OPTIONAL QUESTIONS    The following two questions may be left unanswered but if you do choose
                      to answer them, this will be most helpful to us.  Please note that ALL
                      RETURNED QUESTIONNAIRES WILL BE TREATED AS CONFIDENTIAL.
```

19.	What is your occupation?	Please put a tick here if you
20.	What is your name and address?	would like to talk to the Project Officer about any item
	....	☐

```
THANK YOU FOR ANSWERING THESE QUESTIONS - PLEASE RETURN THIS LEAFLET TO THE PERSON WHO GAVE IT
TO YOU OR DROP IT IN AT THE LIBRARY AT 1 EAST STREET, SOUTH MOLTON.
```

Figure 1   South Molton Library Community Information Project survey (Reproduced by kind permission of Devon Library Services)

make the wording simple and unambiguous, with alternatives spelled out where appropriate, as in the example from South Molton shown here (Fig 1) which was used to establish the need for a multi-agency information and advice service in a small market town in Devon.

When Terence Brake set up a community information service at South Hackney School in London, he rightly surmised that many of the pupils would not understand or use the term 'information' and some might even react with hostility to an emotive word like 'need'. Consequently, he devised a range of simple questionnaires related to the youngsters' interests, such as the one on leisure time illustrated here (Fig 2), which elicit the information in a less formal way and one with which the young people can identify.

The Need To Know?

Name:
Borough you live in:
Are you: Male ☐ Female: ☐

1. Are you satisfied with the way you spend your leisure time? Yes ☐ No ☐

2. How important are the following in the way you spend your leisure time:

	VERY IMPORTANT	IMPORTANT	NOT IMPORTANT
a. Your parents	☐	☐	☐
b. Your own interests	☐	☐	☐
c. The weather	☐	☐	☐
d. The facilities available (e.g. playing fields, cinemas, etc.)	☐	☒	☐
e. Money	☐	☐	☐
f. Jobs at home (looking after brothers/sisters, etc.)	☐	☐	☐
g. Part-time work	☐	☐	☐
h. Transport	☐	☐	☐
i. Religion	☐	☐	☐
j. Being a girl/Being a boy	☐	☐	☐

Which one of these is the most important? _____

3. Approximately how many hours would you spend:

	WEEKDAYS	WEEKENDS
a. Watching T.V.	_____	_____
b. Listening to Radio	_____	_____
c. In youth clubs	_____	_____
d. Discos	_____	_____
e. Pubs	_____	_____
f. Cinemas	_____	_____
g. Playing musical instruments	_____	_____
h. Listening to records	_____	_____
i. Reading	_____	_____
j. Playing sports	_____	_____
k. Watching sports	_____	_____
l. Hobbies	_____	_____
m. Games (e.g. cards, chess, etc.)	_____	_____
n. Visiting libraries, museums	_____	_____

55

Figure 2 South Hackney School 'The Need to Know' Project questionnaire

The drafting of surveys and questionnaires requires a degree of skill which it is not possible to go into here, but if you would like more information, the following books should help:

Line, Maurice B *Library surveys: an introduction to their use, planning, procedure and presentation*. 2nd ed rev by S Stone. Bingley, 1982.

Moore, Nick *How to do research*. Library Association, 1983.

Gardner, Godfrey *Social surveys for social planners*. Open University, 1978.

Writing plain English. Plain English Campaign, 131 College Road, Manchester M16 0AA, 1980.

The method of distributing your survey questionnaire needs careful attention. Two thousand copies of the South Molton questionnaire were distributed as widely as possible, from such outlets as newsagents, cafés, post offices, branch and mobile libraries, and through community groups. Perhaps because of this, the overall response rate was only 11 per cent, though some outlets were markedly more successful than others. It was found that 'the more directly one is involved in the distribution and collection of the questionnaires, the greater will be the response.'[3]

Ideally, it helps if you can be present when the respondent fills in the form, so that any points or questions not understood can be clarified. Often valuable information is imparted verbally through hints and nuances of conversation that would not be transmitted on paper. However, the ideal is seldom attainable and you may have to be content with mailing out your questionnaire. This obviously saves time but you should not expect a very high response rate. It helps, of course, where you can afford it, to include a reply paid envelope for return of the form. Also, questions will need to be couched in even more unequivocal terms.

Surveys can be a help in pointing you in the right direction or by adding weight to already formative ideas but should not be used on their own, only in relation to evidence obtained by other methods. It is as well to bear in mind that in the act of setting a framework of questions for your survey, you are already, to some extent, determining the response.

(f)   *Analyse enquiry statistics* to see if there is a demand from any particular group of user which requires special attention, such as a separate information service. Your organization may already be operating a more traditional reference or information service. An analysis of its enquiries over a period of time, if these are kept in any detail, or, if not, perhaps a short term detailed monitoring of enquiries, may indicate areas of need not being adequately met. Similarly, an approach to other information and advice agencies covering your area of interest for statistical information about their enquiries might also reveal evidence of an unmet need.

By using some or all of the above methods you should have arrived at an idea of the information needs of your community. However, before making a decision on the kind of service required to meet those needs, it is essential to have as complete a picture of your community as possible. The best way to achieve this is to compile a community profile.

Community profiles
This is a systematic process developed initially by corporate planners and adopted more recently by public librarians to enable them to plan and provide services which meet the needs of a given community. A profile will include:

(a) Statistical data about the population: size, rate of growth, age ranges, sex, marital status, religion, ethnic groups, diseases and mortality, employment, education, housing, etc. Much of this information is obtainable from census documents, supplemented and updated by figures from local authority departments, health authorities, employment centres, police, etc.

(b) Socio-economic information: types of economic activity, community services — statutory, voluntary, private, recreational facilities, meeting places, clubs and societies, etc.

(c) Local issues: redevelopment, unemployment, poor housing, transport problems, racial prejudice, etc.

(d) Residents' viewpoints: letters to press, community newspapers, local radio, action groups, community noticeboards, graffiti, informal discussions with those who come into contact with a wide cross-section of the community, informal contacts in pubs, shops, public meetings, etc.

The important thing to remember in compiling a com-

munity profile is not to rely on one type of information
alone as this will give you a biased view. Try to get a fully
rounded picture by including both statistical data and sub-
jective assessment, official opinion and residents' reactions,
majority and minority viewpoints. Obviously you must
tailor your approach to the kind of community you are
analysing. Community profiles were initially designed for
analysing geographical communities, but the same principles
will apply, though the techniques and sources of information
may vary, if your community is a 'closed' one, such as a
school or organization, or a special group, like elderly or
disabled people.

There are also some spin-offs from compiling a community
profile. If you do decide to go ahead and set up an information service, the information gathered for the profile will
form the basis of your local information file and might also
be made available to your clientele in printed form. The valuable contacts made with individuals and groups will form the
basis for your essential information network.

This is just a brief indication of what comprises a community
profile, if you want more detail, the following may be of
help:

Jordan, Peter and Whalley, E D *Learning about the community: a guide for public librarians.* School of Librarianship,
Leeds Polytechnic, 1977.

'Community analysis and libraries' *Library trends.* Vol 24,
No 3 January, 1976.

Beal, Christina *Community profiling: a practical manual.*
Centre for Research on User Studies, University of Sheffield,
1984.

The following conclusions, taken from the above issue of
Library trends, sum up concisely the right way to approach
the question of who needs an information service:

1 Formal and informal methods . . . are essential both for
   developing a clear and useful picture of "who is out
   there" and for an understanding of what they need/
   want.

2 There is no substitute for direct, active information-
   seeking . . . in order to avoid acting on unsubstantiated
   assumptions about groups of people.

3 Just as different communities will want or need different
   services, different approaches will have to be used . . .

There is no single approach which will always work, but respect and flexibility are always essential.[4]

Remember also that some information needs may not become apparent until after your information service is in operation and it ought, therefore, to be flexible enough to adapt to them. Determining needs is not a once and for all exercise but a continuous process.

What information services already exist?

There is one more step that needs to be taken before you can get down to putting flesh on your ideas and that is to find out if there are any other agencies in your area operating identical or similar services to the one that you are planning. You may, in fact, want to take this step at an earlier stage or you might have found out the information in the course of conducting a community profile (see p17). Either way, it is an important stage that should not be omitted, since it is in nobody's interest to duplicate existing services, especially if there is a crying need in another direction.

Information about existing services in a particular neighbourhood can be collected by means of a questionnaire but this will only give you the bare outlines, it will need to be expanded by a personal visit. The advice given above in the section on surveys and questionnaires (p13) is applicable here. The kind of information you will need to collect about each agency is:

(a) location, premises and equipment, opening hours, how to contact the agency;
(b) staffing, information resources, training;
(c) the agency's activities;
(d) referrals, relationships with other agencies;
(e) the agency's users;
(f) feedback to policy makers;
(g) publicity;
(h) management and funding.

The above list was taken from *Who knows?: guidelines for a review of local advice and information services, and how to publicise them* (National Consumer Council, 1982) which is an excellent guide to conducting such reviews and provides more details under each of these headings.

If it is local agencies that you want to identify and you are not a public library, then try your local library for a start.

Other sources might include the Citizens' Advice Bureau, Council for Voluntary Service, Rural Community Council, Social Services Department, civic information bureau and individuals, eg community workers, social workers. There are also a number of directories of information and advice services, some catering for particular needs or clientele, which may give you a lead to a local service:

Advice services in Wales 2nd ed. Welsh Consumer Council, 1981.

Directory of housing aid and advice centres 3rd ed. Association of Housing Aid, 36 Yewfield Road, London NW10, 1983.

Directory of legal advice and law centres. Legal Action Group, 1983.

Directory of tourist information centres. English Tourist Board, annual — covers England, Scotland, Wales, N Ireland, Isle of Man and Channel Islands.

Disability rights handbook. The Disability Alliance, annual — lists national information and advice services and local DIAL (Disablement Information and Advice Line) centres and other disabled advice centres.

Directory of voluntary counselling and allied services. British Association for Counselling, 1978.

Psycho-sexual problems: a directory of agencies offering therapy, counselling and support. British Association for Counselling, 1978.

Aslib directory of information sources in the United Kingdom. 2 vols. Vol 1: Science, technology and commerce. 5th ed edited by Ellen M. Codlin, 1982; Vol 2: Information sources in the social sciences, medicine and the humanities. 4th ed edited by Ellen M. Codlin, 1980. Aslib.

Directory of independent advice. (Expected publication date early 1984, publisher not yet known. Contact Community Information Project, c/o Bethnal Green Library, Cambridge Heath Road, London E2 Tel. 01-981 6114.)

Directory of educational guidance services, 1982. Advisory Council for Adult and Continuing Education (ACACE), free.

Now that all the spadework has been done, you should have a clearer picture of where there is a need for an information service in your community and the gaps or shortcomings in existing provision. You should also by now have some idea of the strengths and weaknesses of existing information and advice services and so be in a position to make a decision about your own proposed service. There are several choices open:

(a) *Maintain and strengthen the existing situation.* It may be that your community is adequately covered by information services, in which case your efforts might best be channelled towards helping to strengthen and maintain those services. The cost of providing an information service is continually rising and any material support or behind the scenes lobbying to help existing services will usually be more than welcome.

(b) *Extend an existing service.* The solution to meeting the information needs of your community does not necessarily have to be your direct responsibility. It may not be appropriate, anyway, if your staff do not have the training, flexibility, time or independence to provide the kind of service that is required. There may well be an existing information and advice service which is prevented from providing an adequate service or extending its work through badly located premises or lack of funds for staffing, training, information resources, etc. Your organization could make an appreciable difference by:

   i Offering free use of suitable accommodation to relocate the service in a more accessible place for the public;

  ii offering similar accommodation for the location of extension services;

 iii offering the use of mobile service points, where feasible, so that remote areas of the community can be reached;

 iv providing help with staffing or resources, eg you may have staff who can offer a particular subject expertise on a surgery basis or you might be prepared to supply loan collections of more expensive reference materials;

  v providing access points for the public in unserved areas on behalf of the information service, eg by having available postal enquiry forms or providing a direct-line telephone link to the service's central office.

(c) *Co-operate.* Although your analysis may well show that there are gaps or shortcomings in existing provision, that should not be a signal to leap in immediately and set up a new service. At a time of financial stringency, it makes sense to explore first of all the possibilities for co-operation and thus to get a more rational and co-ordinated use of resources. This could take the form of:

i   *Sharing information.* Public libraries, for example, could explore ways of making their extensive information resources more useful to other information and advice services. One way would be to agree to keep and up-date files of local information or produce a directory of local information and advice services. Citizens' Advice Bureaux could offer to make their excellent information file available to other services.

ii *Joint collection, processing and dissemination of information.* Often several information services in a community will be involved simultaneously in collecting local information. This is wasted effort, as the information only needs to be collected once, and causes annoyance to those supplying the information. There is obviously scope for a joint approach like that in Peterborough, where an 'umbrella' organization, the Peterborough Information Group, collects the information on behalf of five agencies (see illus p71). This information is also published by a local newspaper group as part of a free directory delivered to over 70,000 homes in the area.

iii *Shared premises.* There are distinct advantages in several agencies sharing premises, in addition to it being economical. It provides better access for the public who can see a number of agencies in one place without a time-consuming and often expensive runaround. Referral is made easier which is particularly useful in multi-problem cases. There is the possibility of not only shared accommodation but also shared information resources, shared publicity, shared casenotes, etc. Sharing can make the service available for longer hours than one agency on its own could possibly attain.

iv *Support groups.* Co-operation of the kind listed in this section can be fostered by the creation of an 'umbrella' group which brings together all the information services in a particular community or area of interest. Such a group could take on activities like information sharing, joint collection of information, co-operative approach to funding, shared publicity, training and generally creating a greater awareness and understanding of each other's work. Sometimes a number of agencies in an area, who are heavily involved in handling problems of a particular kind and do not have the resources or time to cope adequately with them, can benefit from the creation of a specialist support group which can provide training, research, practical assistance (eg tribunal work), information materials, current awareness services, or expertise in certain areas, such as law, debt counselling, housing, planning, tax, etc.

There are a number of co-operative ventures based on the kind of ideas suggested above. If you would like more details of these, contact the Community Information Project, Bethnal Green Library, Cambridge Heath Road, London E2 (tel 01-981 6114) who will be happy to give any help.

    v *Go it alone.* In the next chapter we shall be looking at the practicalities of setting up an information service if, after careful consideration, you decide to go it alone.

References
1   Ward, John 'Equality of information', *Municipal journal*, 82(20), 17 May 1974, 595.

2   Richards, Jean M., ed. *Rural advice and information: the proof of need — the Coquetdale experiment.* (CAB occasional Papers No 2) National Association of Citizens' Advice Bureaux, 1978.

3   Venner, David G. *South Molton Library Community Information Project: final report for the period March 1980-February 1982 to the British Library Research and Development Department on Project SI/G/346.* Devon Library Services, 1982, 30.

4   Croneberger, Robert and Luck, Carolyn 'Community human information needs'. *Library trends*, Vol 24, No 3 January 1976, 524.

Chapter Two

Setting up the service

You have now reached the stage of having:
- * made a thorough investigation of the information needs of your community;
- * identified where gaps exist in information provision;
- * decided on priorities;
- * consulted with other agencies and individuals; and
- * explored the possibilities of co-operation.

As a result, you have decided to set up your own information service. The next step then is to consider:

What kind of information service?
There are a number of functions which can be performed by an information service, of which the following are the main ones:

i *Self-help*, as the name suggests, requires that users find the answers to their own problems. The information service input is directed towards selecting appropriate materials, re-processing information in a form that can readily be understood, packaging information, and arranging all these materials in a way that is appropriate to the user. This kind of service is most suitable where there is insufficient or lack of trained staff to operate a personal enquiry service, such as a small branch or mobile centre, or for deposit in an unmanned centre. In such cases it is usual for the materials to be assembled and produced by a district or central office.

ii *Support* for other information services or for groups of professional workers, etc. Where there are adequate information services to the public, the greater need may lie in an information service to support the work of other agencies and workers in the field. This could take the form of providing (a) selective dissemination of information (SDI) which, in essence, involves channelling information to meet the expressed subject interests of groups or individuals (see p102 for a more detailed discussion); (b) current awareness services; (c) a register of problems; (d) press cuttings service; (e) loan collections of reference books; (f) publicity and educational materials; and (g) local information.

iii *Information giving* can range from simple directional information to complex, such as eligibility for housing benefit or VAT regulations, and may involve *steering* an enquirer to where further help or advice can be obtained without making contact with the service itself.

iv *Referral*, on the other hand, is a more active form of steering in which a contact or appointment is made for the enquirer with an agency who can help. In some cases, it may be necessary to *escort* the client where they do not have sufficient confidence to make contact with the agency who can help them, may be intimidated by officials, or are likely to have difficulties in explaining their case. It is regrettable, but often true, that representatives of an information service can obtain information from official bodies that is denied or simply not offered to members of the public.

v *Advice* is information tailored to individual need. It can be a fairly neutral activity, such as setting out a course of action or options, from which an enquirer must make his or her choice, or it can involve evaluation of available information or services and help with choosing.

vi *Practical help* with writing letters, form filling or making telephone calls.

vii *Advocacy* is needed where a client is not capable of obtaining the information, services, benefits or justice to which he or she is entitled. A positive identification is made with the client's case, which is then argued in front of officials, tribunals or courts on the client's behalf.

viii *Community education* concentrates more on educating the community as to the services that can help them, their entitlement to benefits or rights under the law, rather than providing an information and advice service on a personal basis.

ix *Community action* can arise out of an analysis of enquiries received when it becomes apparent that there is a lack of a service or facility in the community or a programme exists that is working to the detriment of certain groups of people. The information service plays an active role in precipitating change either by acting itself or alerting individuals and groups to campaign.

x *Outreach*, in this context, is providing information to a wider public than the information service's usual clientele, by such means as newspaper and magazine articles, radio, television, advertising, or viewdata.

xi *Counselling* requires much more time and in-depth probing, although it can at one extreme cover simply the act of lending a sympathetic ear to clients who, in externalising their problems, may thus be better able to face them and arrive at a solution. At its other extreme, counselling can lead on to diagnosis and analysis, with ultimately referral of clients to clinics for treatment. Where casework and diagnosis are involved, then specialized professional skills are needed by the interviewer.

Not all these activities will be appropriate to your organization or the community it is intended to serve. Some organizations, for example, have to be impartial, and therefore are precluded from activities which might be construed as 'political', partisan or taking sides in a dispute.

Although for the purposes of this book the different functions of an information service have been treated separately, in practice such clear distinctions can rarely be made. The process of information-advice-advocacy is often referred to as a 'continuum'. Boundaries are blurred and generally not recognized by users even though in setting up a service limits have to be placed on its actions. Someone seeking information or help with a problem is not really interested in the philosophy of your organization, but in obtaining a satisfactory answer or solution, irrespective of the means used to obtain it. Consequently, some people have argued that it is wrong to set up an information service and attempt to limit its functions to say just giving information or advice but not advocacy, since users' expectations may be raised but not completely satisfied. On the other hand, there are those who argue that something is better than nothing. The decision must be yours but, in setting up a service, you must have a clear idea of what you expect it to achieve and, if it is necessary to set limits, how to deal satisfactorily with cases that need to be taken beyond those limits.

The next decision to be made concerns the structure of your service. Is it going to operate from one central point or from a number of outlets? From a static centre or a mobile unit? Obviously, the decision will depend to a great extent on the nature of your community. If it is a rural one, with small scattered pockets of population, then you may want to consider either using a mobile service point or operating through a network of individuals, eg village contacts.[1] If your community is a 'closed' one, such as a school or an organization, then one static centre is likely to be more appropriate. The structure of an information service whose community covers a large geographical area, nationwide for instance, will need to reflect a greater usage by telephone and post, rather than face to face contact with clientele. A general rule, that has already been given but is worth repeating, is to start modestly, and then expand from a secure base, rather than to overcommit at the start and then have to retreat.

Management of the information service

An information service is set up to meet the needs of a given community and one of the best ways to ensure that it meets this objective is for the community to be represented on its management. A fairly common pattern is for a management committee to be made up of representatives from statutory bodies, the service itself, and from individuals and groups in the community. No one group should dominate the management committee and its chairperson should preferably be neutral. An independent committee is particularly necessary where the information service is a non-statutory one whose funding, nevertheless, comes largely from the statutory sector. This is in order to guarantee that undue pressure is not exerted by the funding bodies on the way the service operates. It may be more difficult for an information service belonging to a statutory organization to have an independent management committee, although there is a kind of precedent in the way that state schools each have a Board of Governors made up of representatives of local authorities, parents and staff. Even if a management committee cannot be achieved, some kind of advisory group representing users would be helpful. The responsibilities of a management committee or advisory group might include:

* laying down rules for the use of the service (Fig 3);
* monitoring use and recommending changes;
* suggesting new strategies or areas of work;
* ironing out trouble spots;
* taking community action where lack of provision or malpractice is identified by the information service;
* lobbying for funds or improved facilities;
* giving specialist advice and help on such matters as budgeting, publicity, law, etc.

What is needed to start an information service

Establishing and operating an information service requires certain resources:

* finance: capital and revenue;
* facilities: premises and equipment;
* personnel: training, time to make contacts;
* a system for the collection, processing, storage, retrieval and dissemination of information.

(a) *Financial resources* Whether you are setting up an information service from scratch or simply adding another function to an existing service, there are bound to be financial implications. Capital expenditure will be required, where necessary, to provide premises, furniture and equipment. Revenue may be needed to meet staff salaries and travelling expenses; to pay for rent, rates, heating, lighting, water and telephone; to

Lambeth Information Network

RULES FOR THE
EXCHANGE OF INFORMATION
AND MATERIAL

Members undertake so far as possible to make the contents of their libraries, other than confidential material, available to each other and to give assistance in the provision of information.

Members shall be at liberty to decline to supply information or to lend material and further, to limit the period of loan or to restrict its use to consultation on the premises of the member holding the required item.

The anonymity of enquirers will be preserved if requested.

Members shall nominate up to three persons to be responsible for loans and to act as signatories. Requests from persons other than those included in the official List of Authorities for Loans shall not be accepted without formal notification. Member's authorised signatories shall be responsible for ensuring that the rules of the lending organisation are complied with.

Material lent under LINK arrangements shall be returned to the lender on demand or within such period as the lender may specify. Any member failing to comply with this rule may without prejudice to any rights of the lender have his membership of LINK determined.

Members without librarians or information officers shall normally direct their requests to the headquarters of LINK or through the local branch of Lambeth Public Libraries.

Figure 3 Lambeth Public Libraries 'Link' service rules

purchase stationery; and to publicize and promote the service. It is essential, therefore, that a budget is drawn up setting out as accurately as possible the costs involved, so that sources of finance can be identified.

A non-statutory organization setting up an information service for the first time has a number of possible sources of funding:

i *Local authorities*: counties, district councils, parish councils, development corporations are all empowered to make grants for this purpose. They will be the most likely source of substantial continuous funding and the most problematical. Local authority funding has usually to be voted on each year, so an information service reliant on such funding will always be living on a knife-edge. Changes in the political control of a council can often spark off a reappraisal of support for services. Then local authorities have an annoying habit of trying to influence the policies of organizations they fund, even where these are independent. Many an information service has had to close down because its funding was withheld by the authority who disapproved of actions taken by the service.

Local authorities can also give grants for capital items — premises, furniture and equipment. Some will use their lotteries fund for this kind of grant, but not for revenue funding. If you cannot get funding from the local authority, they may be prepared to give support in kind, such as the provision of premises (short-term accommodation) or shared accommodation in one of its own buildings, eg library, community centre. The most likely local authority departments to approach are social services, leisure and amenities, libraries or education. Look out too for officers with titles like 'Community Development Officer' or 'Youth and Community Officer' who can advise you on what kinds of financial help are available. Your local Council for Voluntary Service (CVS) or Rural Community Council (RCC) may be able to advise you on the right approach to local authorities.

ii *Urban aid* Where a proposed information service is located in a deprived urban area, it may be possible to get an urban aid grant under the government's Urban Programme. You will need to be sponsored by a local authority, who must provide 25 per cent of the funding, and in some cases, by the local Council for Voluntary Service or Rural Community Council who co-ordinate submissions from the voluntary sector. Each local authority will submit up to about ten schemes, including both its own and those from voluntary groups, listed in order of priority, so the first hurdle is to get your scheme as high on the list as possible. The criterion for assessing bids is the degree of social need and if your proposal can demonstrate that it would help to alleviate this, then it will stand a better chance of being viewed favourably. Grants cover both capital expenditure and running costs and can last up to five years. The details of how to apply are set out in a Circular issued by the Department of the Environment each year, usually in the summer. Copies of the Circular are sent to all local authorities and the national headquarters of many voluntary organizations, if you cannot get access to one from either of these sources, it can be purchased from any Government bookshop. There is a very good article on the Urban Programme in *NCVO information service* No 94, June 1983, 15-18.

iii *The Development Commission* gives grants similar to urban aid for projects, including information and advice services, which benefit rural areas. The Commission was set up by the government to administer the Development Fund, which is used to finance any scheme which will improve the rural economy in England. It has a particular interest in depopulated areas and their regeneration. The address is Development Commission, 11 Cowley Street, London SW1 (tel 01-222 9134).

iv *Other government departments* and quangos give grants for specific purposes but are too numerous to list here. A useful book to get hold of or borrow which covers all the various ways of getting money out of the government is *Raising money from government*. Directory of Social Change, 1981, £2.95.

v *Manpower Services Commission* (MSC) has a number of special programmes to help the unemployed which might be suitable for an information service proposal. Funding can cover both capital items, running costs and salaries. Drawbacks are that finance is usually for a limited period and also the Commission from time to time changes the schemes and the rules at the whim of the government, not always for the better. Details of MSC schemes are set out in the book listed at the end of the last section and also in MSC leaflet *Jobs, training and early retirement: government schemes that can help* available free from Jobcentres.

The National Council for Voluntary Organizations produces information sheets and even packs on MSC schemes which can usually be obtained free from them at 26 Bedford Square, London WC1B 3HU.

vi *Local and national trusts* are a useful source of funding for capital expenditure items but are less likely to provide revenue expenditure except for innovative or experimental projects. Charities and trusts often have rules concerning what kind of project they can support. It is useful if you can find out what these are before writing, for a little re-drafting of your proposal could make it more acceptable. District Councils are supposed to keep a list of local charitable trusts and their terms of reference, but failing that, the CVS or RCC will usually be happy to advise on possible sources of local funding. National trusts are listed in *The directory of grant-making trusts*, an annual publication from the Charities Aid Foundation which lists trusts by their area of interest. You should find a copy in the reference section of most major public libraries. A recent development, that is likely to increase, is the establishment of Community Trusts. These are independent bodies who receive money from a variety of sources — trusts, industry, local government — and give grants to voluntary projects. Applications may have to be siphoned first through the local CVS or RCC.

Some helpful advice on raising money from trusts can be found in:

Norton, Michael *Raising money from trusts.* Directory
of Social Change, 1981, £2.95.
Fundraising and grant aid for voluntary organisations.
NCVO, 1982, £1.00.

vii *Other sources* of finance worth considering are industry and the British Library. Industry is hardly
likely to provide substantial funding, and certainly
not for running costs, unless it is an information
service from which they are likely to benefit, such as
a technical and commercial information service or
one providing information for small businesses. In
which case, the kind of support usually forthcoming
will be in the form of an annual subscription, although
you might be able to get help with equipment, eg
microcomputers, duplicators, etc. The kind of help
that industry is likely to give to other kinds of information service will mainly consist of small grants for
equipment or donations of equipment. Try an approach to local firms who manufacture equipment
that you need or explore the possibilities of redundant
typewriters or duplicators now that word processors
have taken over!

The British Library Research & Development
Department has given support in recent years for
innovative information services, eg South Hackney
School 'Right to Know' project and South Molton
Community Information project. If your information
service proposes to break new ground then you may
be able to interest the BL in a research proposal.
It would, however, need to cover the research element
of the work. Only in exceptional circumstances has
the BL provided financial help towards the setting up
and running costs of projects. The address to write to
is The Director, The British Library Research &
Development Department, 2 Sheraton Street, London
W1V 4BH (tel 01-636 1544).

Although most of the possible sources of funding listed
above are for either capital items or relatively short-term
running costs and do not solve the question of how to keep
the information service going in the long term, nevertheless,
they do make it possible to get services off the ground, to

establish them on a sound footing and to demonstrate their worth to the community. Hopefully, then, this will attract more secure and lasting financial support.

An information service that is intended to be simply an extension of an existing statutory service will still need to be costed and the effect on other parts of the service assessed. It is highly unlikely, in these days, that there will be spare capacity, either finance, staff or accommodation, lying around waiting to be used. A sufficiently well thought out and argued scheme might attract additional funding from the authority or via urban aid, but the most likely scenario is that it will have to be provided out of the existing budget. This then means that some kind of re-assessment of current services must take place, in order that priority be given to the proposed information service, and resources be diverted to support it. It hardly needs to be said that for such a process to take place and be successful, both senior management and staff on the ground need to be convinced of the value of the new service and committed to its development.

(b) *Facilities*

    i *Location* The choice of a suitable location for your information service will depend to a certain extent on what can be afforded and on the community you will be serving. If you already have suitable premises with spare capacity which can be used, this will help keep costs to a minimum but, if not, you will need to look elsewhere. It is always a good principle to try to locate an information service where it will be most accessible to its users. Even in a 'closed' community, such as a school or organization, there may be parts of the building that are natural congregating points, eg hall, refectory, social/recreational rooms, coffee machine. Obviously, the location of an information service which does not deal directly with clients, but mainly via the telephone and post, is less crucial. A recent review of research into the use of advice centres[2] suggests that most people use them because they are familiar and very local. They also tend to use those which are near where they live in preference to those which are near where they work. So the ideal location for an information centre that is to serve the public is likely to be in the neighbourhood shopping area. This will not only make it accessible for the purposive user but should also encourage casual use, especially if it has windows in which colourful displays can be mounted. Such locations, however, can rarely be afforded by one agency alone. If a suitable property in such a location becomes available, an alternative would be to consider sharing with several agencies. Sometimes, where an area has been designated for redevelopment, the local authority buys up property, including shops, as it becomes vacant and may be willing to let this to a voluntary organization on a short term basis for a nominal rent. And short terms have the habit of being extended. Enquire at your District Council about property of this kind and also about any premises which may have been empty for some time.

If obtaining your own prominently sited premises, either alone or shared, is out of the question, then consider the possibility of being housed by another organization that already has premises in a suitable location, such as a library, council offices, nearly-new shop or even a commercial concern. Failing that, then the next best thing is to seek for premises where there is a significant traffic flow, even though it may not be with shops, for example near a popular bus stop, a school or clinic, on the way to a shopping centre, or in premises which regularly attract a large number of people eg a community centre, library, health clinic or day centre.

An information service intended to help those with special needs, such as disabled or elderly people, might be best located in a place where they already meet for other purposes — a day centre or handicapped workshop.

Other features to look out for in locating an information service are:
* ground-floor accommodation for ease of access, especially for elderly and disabled people;
* prominent location — not tucked away in a back room or having rear access;

* facilities for display, such as a large picture window;
* informal atmosphere — some buildings may look too 'official' or have unpleasant associations and this can be a deterrent;
* drop-in facility so that potential users, especially the more timid, have a legitimate reason for going into the centre for the first time to 'suss it out' and possibly leave without being challenged.

ii *Space* The space requirements for your information service will depend very much on the type of activities it will be undertaking (see pp25-27). A *self-help service* makes little demand on office accommodation or even an enquiry desk, but will require a prominent location near the major traffic flow and space for notice boards and leaflet/display racks. A *support service* or one that does not deal face-to-face with clientele may only need an office in any habitable location with space for processing materials. A solely *information-giving service* dealing directly with the public, such as a tourist information centre or public library community information service, will perhaps need a waiting/browsing area that is welcoming and relaxing, space for leaflet display and noticeboards, an enquiry desk prominently sited near to major traffic flow, and an office/workroom for the staff. An *advice/counselling service*, in addition to the above, will need an interview room(s) for those clients who need privacy. Some information and advice services put more emphasis on informality and seek collective solutions to problems through group discussion, rather than a one-to-one approach. Here, the centre becomes more a social facility, encouraging people to drop in for a cup of tea or coffee and a chat, out of which information and advice needs can arise incidentally. This style of operation calls for a kitchen or, at least, space where drinks can be made, and a comfortable lounge-type area. An interview room is still necessary for those clients who prefer privacy.

iii *Furniture and equipment*
* *Desks, tables and chairs* The importance of the enquiry desk being located near the main traffic

flow has already been stated. It should be immediately visible on entering the building and clearly labelled. Where the location is unfavourable, this can be overcome to some extent by good signing. The desk should be low and form the least possible barrier between the information seeker and the information staff. It will need to have a fairly large surface area to enable card files, telephone and possibly frequently used quick reference books to be placed on it. Drawers would be useful for pens, stationery, frequently used information files and cash (where the service has items for sale). A chair will be required for the use of the staff, preferably one that is adjustable if more than one person is going to use it, and with a swivel where the staff need to turn around frequently to consult shelves or noticeboard. There should also be a comfortable chair for clients at the enquiry desk and others nearby for those waiting to use the service, with possibly a low coffee table and some magazines for browsing while they wait.

An information service that handles a high voiume of very quick enquiries, like a tourist information centre, might find it more convenient to have a higher bar-type counter with enquirer and staff either standing or using barstools.

* *Telephone* This is likely to be the most important item of equipment in your information service for the staff and the public. Some information services conduct most of their business with clients over the telephone. In such cases, where it is desirable to link a telephone enquirer immediately with another service, this can be achieved by means of a three-way or conference line facility. The most useful location for the telephone is on the enquiry desk, though further lines or extensions may be required in the interview room or office. Opinions differ as to the desirability of having telephones in interview rooms. In some instances, when seeking information or trying to sort out a problem on behalf of a client with another organization, it can be helpful to have the client by the 'phone so that

points can be clarified as soon as they arise. On the other hand, there will be occasions when you will want to talk frankly to another organization without the client overhearing, in which case it is better if the telephone is located in a private office. Ideally, both options should be available but if this is not possible, then you will have to decide on the basis of which will cause the least inconvenience.

Where possible, your information service should have its own separate telephone line so that clients can make contact direct without having to go through a switchboard or waiting for lines to become available. If that is not possible, then an extension exclusively for the information service is the next best thing. It is helpful if you can obtain a telephone number that is easily remembered by users.

There are several instances where people living in more remote areas have been provided with free telephone access to a central information service through the installation of a direct line from a local public building, eg a branch library. This has been used as an alternative to providing an extension bureau or to compensate for the withdrawal of local offices. The main space requirements would be for a sound-proof booth or office.

You may consider that it is important for your information service to be able to offer help outside its normal opening hours. In which case you will need to instal a telephone answering machine, so that at any hour of the day or night when the service is closed, enquirers can leave messages. More sophisticated answering machines also enable you to record a message or information which is played back to callers when they ring the service. The kinds of information which might be appropriate to record in this way are contacts for emergency services, hotel vacancies, caravan/camping sites, bus or train times, etc.

* *Card files* Unless you are in the fortunate position of being able to afford a microcomputer (see p76), it is most likely that your information file will

be contained on cards, the most popular sizes being 5in × 3in and 8in × 5in. These cards will need to be housed either in drawers in a wooden or metal cabinet or in open boxes/drawers (wooden or cardboard). The cheapest method if you are really operating on a shoestring is to beg some empty boxes from a local shoe shop or a decent looking shallow wooden crate from the greengrocer which can be divided by some simple partitions. Open cardboard boxes designed for card filing are fairly cheap and can be found at most office equipment suppliers. Open wooden boxes are much more expensive so why not try to knock up some from offcuts of wood? They don't need to be very sophisticated or load-bearing. Open boxes are easy to use and display the information clearly but they also have some disadvantages: they cannot be stacked one on top of the other; they are open to dust, drips from coffee cups, discarded chewing gum and other unmentionable objects; and, if knocked over, the cards spill out and you have the tiresome job of re-filing them again.

Card drawers overcome these problems even if the information is slightly less accessible. Again, you can get cheap drawers made of cardboard or expensive ones in wood but the most common type is the two drawer metal filing cabinets (Fig 4). Each drawer holds approx. 1,000 cards and, if you need greater capacity now or later, units can be stacked one on top of the other. Some drawers have a rod which holds the cards in place but this can be a nuisance if you need to take cards out frequently for up-dating or have information on the back of cards. For even greater storage capacity you will need to consider a free-standing metal or wooden cabinet but these are rather expensive items. With more and more public libaries going over to microfiche or computer catalogues, there may well be an opportunity to pick up such a cabinet at a knock-down price. Enquire at your local public library — but don't mention my name!

Figure 4 The Myers-Kingsbury range of steel card index cabinets

There are on the market other more sophisticated files which usually have their own specially shaped cards. If you decide to buy one of these, you will need to take account not only of the cost of the equipment but also the continuing cost of the specialised stationery. The systems described previously use standard sizes, so that it is possible to use scrap cards or print your own with a pre-determined grid to save costs. One card unit that does have some useful features is the Rondofile (Fig 5) which, as its name suggests, works on a turntable system. The file is spun round to consult an appropriate card and cards are easily removed for amendment or adding to. Cards are also available in a variety of colours, so it is possible to introduce an elementary colour-coding of information, say by area, subject or type of organization. A Rondofile is compact enough to be housed on the enquiry desk and thus can be accessible to both public and staff. One file holds 1,000 cards and, if more capacity is required, a second unit can be stacked on top. For details and up-to-date prices of Rondofiles contact M Myers & Sons Ltd, PO Box 16, Vicarage Street, Langley Green, Oldbury, Warley, West Midlands B68 8HF (tel, 021-552 3322).

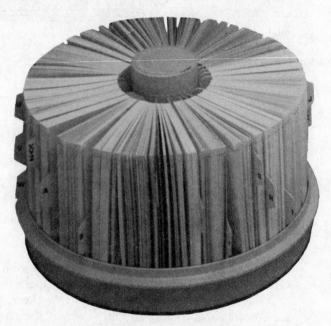

Figure 5 Myers Rondofile 600.

A similar card filing system using a vertical rotary action is made by Rotadex Systems Ltd, 3/5 Fortnum Close, Kitts Green, Birmingham B33 0JL. (Fig 6) There are twenty-four models in the range suitable for five different card sizes, the largest housing 9,000 cards.

Many office equipment suppliers have these systems in stock.

* *A filing cabinet* and dividers will be needed for keeping flimsy publications such as pamphlets, leaflets, broadsheets, posters, etc which provide valuable information for your service. Cabinets come in one, two, three or four drawer units usually in metal, though there are some cheap cardboard ones on the market. At a pinch you can always make do with cardboard cartons and used manilla envelopes.

* *Bookshelves* Virtually every information service will have some books to refer to, varying from a mere handful to many hundreds of volumes. Small numbers can be kept on the enquiry desk itself using bookends (any heavy weight or 'posh' commercial ones), a bookslope or one of those coiled spring contraptions. Slightly more can be housed conveniently on a book trolley and sited

Figure 6   Rotadex Rotary Vertical Card Filing Unit

near the desk for quick reference. Larger numbers will require some form of book shelving, even if it is only cardboard or wooden cartons laid on their side or planks suspended across house bricks. There are numerous varieties of commercially-made metal and wooden shelving available from library furniture and equipment suppliers, your local public library will help you with addresses. For

cheapness, though, try industrial metal shelving; Habitat do a 'domesticated' version in bright, gay colours.
* *Noticeboards* will be needed to display posters and information sheets for your clientele. Rarely does an information service have sufficient noticeboard space, so be generous in your estimate where funds allow. For cheapness, buy a large sheet of pin-board and cut to size to fill empty wall spaces, pillars, etc. Boards do not need to have too smart a finish since most of the time they will be covered with posters. A noticeboard standing or hanging in a window of your centre and visible to the public can be used to advertise special events taking place, surgeries, or information that could be of use when the centre is closed. Alternatively, consider using a blackboard or an external wall-mounted noticeboard for this purpose. External noticeboards are best covered, using vandal-proof glass or perspex.
* *Leaflet racks or dispensers* Considering the vast number of leaflets of all shapes and sizes that are available, the choice of ready-made equipment for displaying them is not brilliant and what does exist is often expensive. All the more reason for trying to make your own. Here are two cheap suggestions: (i) Cut stiff manilla envelopes of the size required to make pockets, glue them in rows on a large piece of card and pin this onto a wall or noticeboard. An alternative material to use for pockets is adjustable book jacketing which has an added advantage in allowing all the leaflet to be seen through the plastic front. (ii) Screw cup hooks into a sheet of blockboard or similar material and hang leaflets from them by punching a hole in the top. A copy of the leaflet cover pasted onto the board will act as an 'aide memoire' when stocks have all been taken.

A fairly cheap and attractive stick-on or free-standing leaflet dispenser made of polypropylene and available in all the standard sizes is manufactured by Mainline Marketing Ltd, 2a Bank Street,

Figure 7 Mainline leaflet dispensers

Tonbridge, Kent TN9 1BL. (Fig 7) Only one colour, chocolate brown, is available ex-stock, but a variety of colours can be supplied to order, including overprinting and multiple dispensers on one sheet. There are similar individual leaflet fittings which attach to Marler Haley Expoloop display boards (see next section for details).

C & J Murrell Ltd, Field Road, Mildenhall, Suffolk do a variety of fairly cheap white plastic coated wire leaflet and pamphlet racks suitable for various locations: table, wall or free-standing. Their most versatile is a free-standing gondola unit with interchangeable sides to take A4, A5 or 1/3A4 size leaflets. Unfortunately, this is not available ex-stock with a choice of sides, only with 1/3A4 sides. However, Murrell's do supply the English Tourist Board with the variable version and, so far, they have been willing to supply other centres as well as Tourist Information Centres with them. Write to English Tourist Board, 4 Grosvenor Gardens, London SW1 0DU for details.

If money is no problem then you would, perhaps, be better off with a custom made leaflet dispenser. The one shown here (Fig 8) was constructed quite cheaply by a school woodwork department but it should be within the capabilities of any moderately competent do-it-yourselfer.

Figure 8 Leaflet display rack at Orton District Library, Peterborough

* *Display boards* will be needed if you intend to put on free-standing exhibitions or displays. There are

innumerable makes available in a variety of price ranges, many offering special features or accessories. It would pay you to look around first and get advice from someone in the know, such as the publicity officer of a local authority, large firm or other undertaking.

If any display boards can be said to be universal, then it must be those of Marler Haley Exposystems Ltd, who do several different systems at moderate prices that are easy to erect, versatile and attractive. They also have a range of useful accessories like shelves, lights, leaflet dispensers, etc which go with the boards. Write to them for details and prices at 7 High Street, Barnet, Herts EN5 5UE.

A cheap display system to meet the needs of charities and small organizations has been designed by Tony Othen & Associates (Fig 9). It is made of a corrugated plastic material, lightweight, easy and quick to put up, capable of being erected in a variety of ways, and available in several colours. Details and prices from them at Neptune House, 70 Royal Hill, Greenwich, London SE10 8RT.

* *Sloping shelves* may be needed for displaying magazines, leaflets or information packs face outwards. Most modern library shelving systems have facilities to accommodate sloping shelves. Ask at your local public library for addresses of suppliers. Books for Students, Catteshall Lane, Godalming, Surrey GU7 1NG do a cheap blockboard and plastic unit that has three slopes and fits any standard 3ft shelf. Murrell's also have a cheap sloping shelf unit (see section on Leaflet racks above for address).

* *Strip indexes* are an alternative to card files for recording local information (Fig 10). They are limited as to the amount of information that can be contained on a strip, although a variety of widths is available. Strips are more awkward to interfile and update but they have the advantage that it is possible to photocopy quite easily the whole file or sections on demand. Kalamazoo do a variety of holders and strips but these are

Figure 9 Tony Othen & Associates display system

a little expensive. Their address is Kalamazoo Business Systems, 1 Market Street, Bromsgrove, B61 8EP.

A cheaper line is available from Datex Systems, Brandsby, York YO6 4SJ.

Figure 10 Datex Slipstrip Index

* *Other furniture and equipment* It is possible to list a great many more items of furniture and equipment that an information service might need, depending on the nature of the service, the resources available, and the existence or otherwise of back-up secretarial help. I will simply note a few items that may be considered: (a) pigeonholes for storing leaflets, (b) bench or flat surface for assembling packs or publications, (c) typewriter, (d) photocopier, (e) machine for recording users/enquiries ('clicker'), (f) duplicator — stencil or offset. A range of reasonably cheap storage and filing units for cards and documents is made by Neat Ideas Mail Order (formerly Bankers Box Liberty), Sandall Stones Road, Kirk Sandall Industrial Estate, Doncaster DN3 1HT who will supply a catalogue on request.

iv *Stationery*
   * *Pamphlet boxes* will be needed for storing booklets, leaflets and other ephemeral materials for use by

staff or clientele. They are available in several sizes and quality, from cardboard to plastic, closed and open at the top. If you are really hard up, try breakfast cereal cartons! Sometimes new reference books come in strong slip cases which make excellent storage boxes. Lawtons Ltd, 60 Vauxhall Road, Liverpool L69 3AU do a cheap A4 size cardboard pamphlet box, called the Lawco Box, which comes flat and is then folded into shape. A more up-market A4 fold-up file box in brightly coloured plastic-covered card is produced by Esselte Dymo Ltd, Spur Road, Feltham, Middlesex TW14 0SL. The same firm also has a polystyrene plastic pamphlet magazine file box (Fig 11) in bright colours, sizes A4 and A5, if money's no object. The 'Gruyère cheese' see-through sides can be annoying when replacing items, as the corners tend to catch in the holes.

* *Manila folders and envelopes* to file cuttings, leaflets, information sheets in the vertical filing cabinet. Plastic wallets are even better if you can afford them as they enable the contents to be immediately visible. They are particularly useful if you want to go in for compiling information packs for your clients. I have never been able to find any of these off-the-peg, though I am sure they must exist. Celsur Plastics Ltd (address p118) will make these to your specifications.

* *Cards* — 5in × 3in for subject indexes or brief information. Use scrap cards for cheapness. 8in × 5in cards for recording more detailed information about organizations and services. Can be overprinted with a standard grid for entering information.

* *Forms, headed paper, standard letters* for collecting information, press releases, etc.

* *Notepads* printed with your logo, opening hours and services (see Fig 26) on which to write information for enquirers. Acts as a form of publicity for the service.

* *Statistics sheets* for gathering information about the use made of the service (see pp139-143).

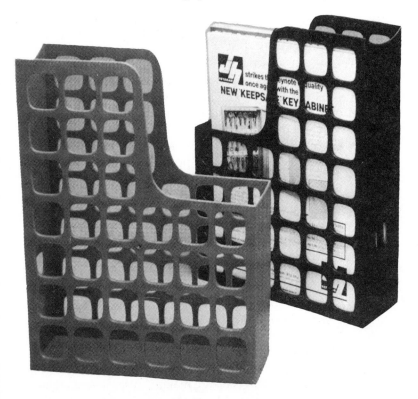

Figure 11 Esselte Boxer Magazine Files

(c)   *Staff* Although staff resources have been left till last
they are, in fact, the most important element of an information service. However efficient and comprehensive the
information gathering system and sophisticated the equipment, if the staff are not, to borrow a piece of computer
jargon, 'user friendly' then your service will not attract
customers. A bright, helpful and sympathetic person can
more than make up for limited resources, so it pays to concentrate on getting the right one or ones. The right one, in
this instance, may not necessarily be the person who is most
qualified academically or professionally. The important
characteristics being a commitment to the aims of the information service and an approachable personality.

It is not possible to lay down any formula regarding the
staffing of an information service because there are so many

variables. An information service that is merely an extension of an already existing service may be able to make use of the same staff, given that they have sufficient spare capacity, are in sympathy with the aims of the new service and, where necessary, have been adequately trained. Avoid loading extra work onto an already hard-pressed staff as this can cause resentment and will not help to ensure the success of the service. Make sure also that the administrative and clerical services will be able to cope with the increased demands made by the service (see chart on pp52-53). It may be that in order to take on a new function, some aspects of the existing service will have to decline or be dropped altogether. Again, it is important to get the staff committed to these changes from the beginning and not to present them as a 'fait accompli' without discussion.

If you are starting an information service from scratch, then a decision will have to be made whether it is to be run by full or part-time staff, volunteers, or through a Manpower Services Commission job creation programme or a combination of any of these. Either way, the first priority will be to obtain a suitable person to organize the service. Such a person will need to have a hand in selecting staff, recruiting volunteers, arranging training, publicising the service, setting up the information system and making sure that adequate records are kept. Prepare a job description for the post and, if it is to be a paid appointment, set the salary and hours for work (see Appendix One for a specimen job description). To find out what salary to offer, check adverts in appropriate periodicals or newspapers for similar posts, approach other information services of a similar type, or contact the umbrella organization, if there is one, for your type of service (see Appendix Two for list of addresses). Even where the organizer's post is to be a voluntary one, the degree of commitment expected should warrant a small payment or honorarium. Make it quite clear to whom the organizer is responsible. There is a useful book produced by Voluntary Action Westminster called *The 'Job evaluation' kit* which is intended to help local voluntary organizations decide on appropriate salaries for their paid staff. Copies can be obtained from them at 1 St Mary's Terrace, London W2 1SU.

The number of staff or volunteers you require will depend on the information service you are planning, the opening hours, and the volume of work expected. Opening hours must take account of the needs of your community and the interests of the staff. Long opening hours obviously make the service more accessible, but the staffing requirement may be too great for the resources available. Staff also like to be kept busy, long periods of inactivity can be demoralizing unless there is 'housekeeping' work that can be done in between enquiries. It is best to aim initially for modest opening hours chosen to suit likely patterns of most usage and availability of staff or volunteers. You can always expand or adjust in the light of experience and more staffing. The review of research into the use of advice services mentioned earlier (p35) has shown that there is a sort of threshold of opening hours. Once the threshold is passed, the increase in use is proportionately greater than the increase in hours. If your service is aimed at the public, try to get a mixture of hours – day, evening, lunchtime, Saturday – so that as many people as possible have a chance to visit the service.

The table below sets out some of the main activities undertaken by the staff of each type of information service who are either in direct contact with clientele, working behind the scenes in a supporting role, or providing clerical/secretarial services. In practice, of course, there may not be such a clear division of responsibilities and you could well find all three categories performed by one person. However, the table may be a help in working out the number of staff required.

As well as sufficient staff to cover the hours your service is open, you will also need to make allowances for sickness, holidays, training and other unforeseen disasters. So don't rely on just one person, there should always be adequate back-up staff. Most full-time workers only actually work about 200 days each year once allowance is made for weekends, holidays and sick leave.

Volunteers
Volunteers can be a great asset in running an information service, indeed some services exist entirely on voluntary help, provided they are of the right calibre and are suitably trained. In recruiting volunteers, it will help to draw up a brief job description of the type of work you expect them to do and the kind of personality you are looking for. You may be overwhelmed with enquiries, since information and advice

TYPES OF SERVICE	STAFF FUNCTIONS		
	DIRECT CONTACT WITH INDIVIDUALS AND GROUPS	SUPPORT	CLERICAL
SELF HELP	(a) Simple directional enquiries and referral (b) Tidying self-help section (c) Maintaining leaflet and poster displays	(a) Identification and selection of appropriate materials (b) Organization of self-help collections (c) Preparation of self-help materials — leaflets, packs, etc (d) Up-dating of self-help collections and packs	(a) Typing of self-help information lists and leaflets (b) Duplicating/printing of same
SUPPORT	(a) Regular contact with groups to identify needs (b) Help with classifying and arranging information files and collections (c) Training in retrieval and organization of information	(a) Selection and assembling of materials for loan collections (b) Scanning of periodicals etc for SDI, bulletin, press cuttings services (c) Preparation of same (d) Collecting and organizing local information (e) Preparation of publicity/educational materials	(a) Sending out standard letters (b) Typing of information file entries, bulletins leaflets, etc (c) Duplicating/printing of same

STAFF FUNCTIONS

TYPES OF SERVICE	DIRECT CONTACT WITH INDIVIDUALS AND GROUPS	SUPPORT	CLERICAL
INFOR-MATION	(a) Information-giving to individuals or groups either face-to-face, by 'phone or post (b) Maintaining leaflet and poster displays (c) Selling publications, tickets, etc (d) Booking accommodation	(a) Researching difficult enquiries (b) Collecting, organizing and up-dating information files (c) Selection of books, pamphlets, etc (d) Preparation of information guides, packs, etc (e) Publicity for service — posters, leaflets, radio/TV spots, etc (f) Preparation of displays	(a) Typing of letters in reply to postal enquiries (b) Typing of information file cards (c) Sending standard letters (d) Typing of information guides, etc (e) Duplication/printing of same
ADVICE ADVOCACY, COUNSEL-LING	All activities listed under INFORMATION above, plus: (a) Giving advice on a one-to-one basis (b) Contributing to group discussion of problems (c) Client reception (d) Escort (e) Maintaining case notes (f) Practical help (g) Representation at tribunals, courts, etc.	All activities listed under INFORMATION above plus: (a) Feedback (b) Preparation of cases for tribunals, etc (c) Scanning of periodicals for useful articles and case notes, etc	All activities listed under INFORMATION above plus: (a) Typing letters on behalf of clients (b) Typing tribunal case notes

work is generally regarded as being a very worthwhile and
satisfying activity because it is varied, interesting and its
effects are often immediately recognizable. Not everyone,
however, will be suited to this kind of work, so you will
need to take care over the selection. Here are some points to
look out for:
   * What time commitment can the volunteer offer? Is it
     flexible? Does it meet the hours your service operates?
   * Does the volunteer have a personality that is approach-
     able and will encourage clients to seek information or
     reveal their problems?
   * Can the volunteer be trusted to keep confidences to
     themselves?
   * How would the volunteer react under pressure?
   * Has the volunteer got initiative and perseverence in
     seeking information?
   * Will the volunteer understand and keep within the rules
     and regulations of your service?
   * Has the volunteer the capacity for training and the
     ability to recall that training in dealing with clients?
   * Has the volunteer the right attitude to accept orders
     and direction from paid workers or other senior
     volunteers?
If you have difficulties in recruiting volunteers on your own,
you can get help from your local Council for Voluntary
Service or Rural Community Council. There may even be a
Volunteer Bureau in your town which specializes in finding
and placing volunteers.

Training
Once you have selected your staff and volunteers, you will
need to provide them and subsequent recruits with access to
some form of training, depending on the demands of your
service. At the very least, they will need to have an understanding of why the service has been set up, what it aims to
achieve and how they can help. Beyond that, you have to
decide whether the skills required to operate the service can
be obtained by:
   * formal internal courses
   * informal methods, such as 'sitting next to Nellie'
   * external local courses
   * external national courses

In addition, you will have to consider for existing staff:
* continuous learning
* refresher courses.

Certain information and advice services have their own well-developed training programmes, usually devised by the national organization. Citizens Advice Bureaux have an excellent training scheme devised by their national organization, the National Association of Citizens' Advice Bureaux (NACAB) and for staff of tourist information centres there are regular training courses run by their regional tourist board.

(a) *Formal internal courses.* Organizing your own internal training course has a number of advantages. It can be slanted to the particular needs of the service and the acquisition of basic skills can be practised using the materials and equipment that the recruit will have to hand in operating the service. It can also be combined effectively with practical 'on-the-job' training. Such a course will need to combine formal talks with practical exercises and possibly visits to other information and advice services. Usually 8-10 people is regarded as a minimum for running a formal course. Less than this and you may want to consider using a combination of continuous 'on-the-job' training and external courses or combining with one or more other agencies to provide a joint training scheme.

Model internal training programmes are set out in the following publications and may be useful in planning your own scheme:

Turick, Dorothy *Community information services in libraries.* (Library Journal Special Report no. 5) Library Journal, New York, 1978 66-67.

Jones, Clara S., *ed. Public library information and referral service.* Gaylord Professional Publications, New York, 1978.

(b) *Informal training methods.* 'Sitting next to Nellie' is perhaps the most time-honoured method of imparting practical skills and still one of the most effective. As the name implies, it involves the recruit in sitting alongside an experienced information worker or adviser in order to learn how the job is done. It is probably not sufficient on its own to cover all training requirements and will need to be supplemented by other methods.

(c) *External local courses* If formalized training is required and you do not have sufficient new recruits or the resources to warrant running your own course, then look around at what courses are already on offer in your area. Some Colleges of Further Education run courses in such subjects as welfare rights, for example, often in conjunction with organizations like Child Poverty Action Group or the Workers Educational Association. Some Councils for Voluntary Service or other umbrella groups organize either basic training courses or ones on more specialized topics. Some Citizens Advice Bureaux are now opening up the NACAB training scheme to other information and advice workers. Ask at your local bureau or NACAB regional office for local availability. Training provided by external courses may not exactly match the requirements of your service and will need to be supplemented by some form of internal training.

(d) *External national courses* There is a variety of courses available nationally which provide some training that would be helpful to staff running an information and advice service. These range from academic courses leading to a professional qualification to day courses organized by national campaign organizations. Space will only allow the briefest of details about the kind of courses available.

* *Librarianship courses* cover such subjects as classification, cataloguing, and information retrieval which may be relevant. Courses are run by schools of librarianship usually attached to universities or polytechnics. Some, like Leeds School of Librarianship, have special modules on community informaton, but others see it as just part of the general framework. The Library Association, 7 Ridgmount Street, London WC1E 7AE (tel 01-636 7543) will help with addresses of library schools and advise on library education in general. They also run a number of short courses on topics, some of which may be relevant to information and advice workers, as do Aslib (Association for Information Management), 3 Belgrave Square, London SW1X 8PL (tel 01-235 5050). Contact them for details.

* *Community work courses* — taught at many colleges of various levels. Most courses have optional subjects

that would be relevant to information and advice work, such as welfare rights, housing policy, and law and the community worker.

* *Information and advice work courses* — the excellent Post-Graduate Diploma offered by North East London Polytechnic is alas no more. Birmingham Polytechnic has a part-time certificate course of half a day per week for one academic year in 'Community and Advice Work' — no entrance requirements needed but some practical experience is expected.

* *Voluntary organizations and other bodies* often arrange short courses of interest to information and advice workers. The most well known is the National Association of Citizens' Advice Bureaux training scheme which is usually available on a local or regional basis. Child Poverty Action Group, Legal Action Group, Shelter, National Marriage Guidance Council, Directory of Social Change, Consumers' Association all have national training courses which are widely available. The training is usually aimed at their particular area of interest. The Community Information Project, Bethnal Green Library, Cambridge Heath Road, London E2 (tel 01-981 6114) run a community information course aimed mainly at librarians but they would also be happy to give you advice on other suitable courses.

* *Self-instructors and training packs* — several organizations have produced training packs usually for individuals to work through on their own or in small groups. A good example is NACAB whose packs include *Using CANS* (Citizens' Advice Notes), *Using reference books, Unfair dismissal* and *Undefended divorce self-instructor*. The packs are cheap and availability is not restricted. Details from NACAB, 110 Drury Lane, London WC2B 5SW. Newham Rights Centre's *Citizens' rights course notes* are excellent for training purposes as they include further reading suggestions. Details from Newham Rights Centre, 285 Romford Road, London E7 9HJ. Further examples of training materials for information and advice work are listed in *Know how to find out your rights* by Grainne Morby (Pluto Press, 1982).

Continuous learning and refresher courses

It is essential that staff of an information service are kept up to date on new information and developments, so you will need to devise a system for ensuring this. One way is to organize a regular staff briefing session at a time when the service is not open to its customers. Sessions can be used not only to impart new information but also to discuss recurrent problems, difficult enquiries and newly discovered sources of information. It may not be possible to get all the staff together at one time, especially if the service is run by part-time staff and volunteers. In these instances you could use a bulletin board or regular staff memos/newsletter.

In addition to continuous learning, your staff may need to attend refresher courses, particularly in subjects they need to know about but don't use regularly, and in order to develop new techniques or keep up-to-date in ones already acquired.

The above notes on training owe a lot to an excellent study written by Julia M Reid for a Masters degree at the University of Sheffield Department of Information Studies called *Education and training for community information and advice work* (University of Sheffield Department of Information Studies, 1982). It is not just a theoretical work but has lots of detail about existing training courses, including the reproduction of syllabuses.

Insurance

There are several kinds of insurance which it may be necessary or advisable to take out for the protection of the staff of your information service and the clientele who use it. A service that is part of another organization may well be covered for some of these eventualities but it is best to make sure.

* *Public liability insurance* — sometimes called legal liability or third party insurance — is an essential. It protects you against any claims for injury occurring on the premises and caused by neglicence. Compensation can be as high as £50,000 plus if negligence is proved.

* *Personal accident insurance* is recommended for the protection of staff and volunteers of the service and should cover assault by users of the service, including damage to clothing.

* *Protection against giving wrong advice* is advisable if the service is providing more than straightforward information giving. An information service can be sued for giving wrong advice if it results in the client losing money or suffering harm.

* *Fire, theft and all risks insurance* is needed if you have expensive equipment or your premises are not protected by the insurance of a parent organization.

  For further information on insurance there is a useful booklet published by the National Council for Voluntary Organizations called *Insurance protection: a guide for voluntary organisations and for voluntary workers* (NCVO, 1983, £2 plus 50p p & p).

The other major resource needed by an information service is a system for collecting, processing, storage, retrieval and dissemination of information and that requires a chapter of its own.

References

1   Kempson, Elaine *Village contacts: a guide to setting up a village based advice service.* Community Information Project, 1982.

2   *Patterns of use of advice services: a review of research.* Community Information Project, to be published.

Chapter Three

The information base

Information is the lifeblood of an information service and the information file is its heart. Unless the heart is sound and continually pumping a supply of regularly renewed information into the system, it will not function at its best. Therefore, it is important to give extra care and attention to planning the resources needed to set up a sound information base and a workable system for keeping it up-to-date.

Some basic things you will need to consider are:

    i How is the information to be collected?
    ii What method is to be used for processing and storing information?
    iii How is the information to be retrieved?
    iv What size is the file likely to be?
    v What areas, geographical and subject, is the file to cover?

In addition, you will need to consider how the information is going to be disseminated, but that is a subject for the next chapter.

The kind of system you choose and the degree of its sophistication will depend partly on the nature of your information service and partly on the staff and financial resources available. When designing your information system, make sure it is readily understandable to all the people, part-time volunteers and laypersons included, who will be using it, and not just to professionals.

Coverage
In identifying the need for your information service, you should have reached a decision already on the community to

be served. This may be either a geographical community or a community of interest. Either way, you will still need to make a decision about the extent of your information base. For example, a neighbourhood information service must decide what information to collect on the wider area — county, region, nation — outside its local community. An information service aimed at a fairly wide area may need to limit its interests to a particular sector of the community or to a particular range of subjects. Even an information service in support of a local campaign may benefit from collecting information on similar campaigns or problems countrywide. A service set up to meet the needs of a particular client group, say local commerce and industry, might decide that the greatest need is to provide information for small businesses rather than the major firms who will probably have information services of their own.

Types of information

The information base of your service will most likely include the following types of information:

* *Soft information* — details of clubs, societies, organizations and services; individuals; events; etc. Usually this information will not be available in a published form or, at least, not in sufficient detail and it will be necessary to make a conscious effort to collect it. This information will comprise the major part of the resources file.

* *Hard information* — factual information on a specific subject eg benefit rates for single parent families, how to get legal aid, what items are subject to VAT, or how to change your name. This information will be available in a variety of forms, some ephemeral such as leaflets, pamphlets, booklets, broadsheets, posters, periodical articles, etc. which will need to be kept in a vertical file, in storage boxes or similar receptacles and accessed via some form of index or classification scheme, others such as books, multi-volumed reference works, law books, etc. will need to be classified and shelved.

* *Supplementary information* is information already produced in a particular format — directories, handbooks,

diaries, annual reports, constitutions, newsletters — of organizations appearing in the resources file.

Collecting soft information

It is highly unlikely and undesirable that an information service should need to 'go it alone' on the collection of information. Such is the volume and complexity of information in present-day society that, unless your service has very narrow terms of reference, it will be virtually impossible for it to collect and keep up to date all the information that it requires. Therefore, it is important that you first of all identify the information providers, support services and 'gatekeepers' in your community and establish effective contacts with them. These links may already have been forged in the process of conducting a community profile. They now need to be fostered and strengthened, so that there can be a mutual exchange of information. These contacts will also be able to provide you with useful feedback from the community as to the success or otherwise of your service.

The network of contacts can be maintained on a fairly casual, occasional basis, as the need arises, or you might want to formalize the arrangement. Some ways of doing this include irregular 'get togethers', informal luncheon clubs, regular meetings with agendas and minutes, or the circulation of a newsletter or bulletin. Other activities that could develop out of such meetings are joint collection of information, shared publicity, compilation and publication of directories, information handbooks and leaflets, training and general discussion of common problems.

Collecting information is a time consuming process and there is no one method of going about it. You will probably have to use a combination of several techniques to build up a satisfactory information base. One thing definitely to be avoided is duplicating work that has already been done. So first of all:

   i *Identify existing information files* by contacting all the other information services, council departments and organizations who are likely to maintain information files and ask if they would be willing to share this information. Try to offer something in return, either an exchange of information or some other help help you can provide. Next check:

ii *Local directories* There are several types of directory
that may be available in your area and which are
useful as sources of soft information: (a) local government authorities often produce directories or town
guides of their area, usually to encourage tourism or
industry, which contain a certain amount of local
information; (b) telephone directories, especially
Yellow Pages which have an alphabetical subject
arrangement; (c) area directories, such as those produced by Thompson's Newspapers, which are similar
to Yellow Pages but also contain a section of community information. Some local newspaper groups,
like the East Midlands Allied Press, have produced
such directories in conjunction with local information groups (Fig 12); (d) citizens' guides may also
be produced by the local press but as supplements to
an existing newspaper (Fig 13); (e) Councils for
Voluntary Service or Rural Community Councils
sometimes produce directories of voluntary organizations in their area; (f) directories covering a special
subject, such as accommodation, halls for hire, etc;
(g) directories aimed at a particular interest group or
groups eg places of worship, access for the disabled,
senior citizens handbooks, Chamber of Commerce
directory, etc.

iii *National directories* Useful not only for the wider
network of services but also for identifying local
offices of a national organization. See page 20 for a
list of some of these and also Grainne Morby's book
Know how to find out your rights (Pluto Press,
1982). Other methods to use in building up your
information base and maintaining its currency include:

iv *Looking and listening* A lot of information can be
gathered by simply walking around your community,
looking at notice boards, picking up leaflets, or
attending open meetings, fairs, fetes and other community events. This method of collecting information is unpredictable and requires more than a
five-day week, 9-5 involvement.

v *Contact with individuals* People are a major source of
information in any community and there are always

Council services — Peterborough

The old city of Peterborough and the surrounding area is governed jointly by Peterborough City Council and Cambridgeshire County Council, both of which came into being as a result of local government re-organisation in April 1974.

The city council now has 48 councillors who annually elect a mayor from among their number.

The city council is responsible for planning, housing, some roads, environmental health, recreation and leisure facilities.

The county council looks after education, social services, county strategic roads, police, the fire service, libraries and consumer protection.

Both councils have offices at a variety of locations. For ease of reference, services provided by both councils are listed below in strictly alphabetical order, with the address and telephone number to contact if you have a query.

Architects' Department

City Architect: Mr W J H Greenwood, 80 Lincoln Road, Peterborough. Tel 63141.
This department is responsible for the building programme of the city council, together with the maintenance of public buildings. Other areas of responsibility include an advisory service on building costs, building design, construction and graphics.

Community Development

This service includes the development, provision and maintenance of community centres and halls, adventure playgrounds, and the promotion of children's holiday playschemes. A small team of community workers and playleaders is available to help local groups to assess and meet their needs.
Community development officer: Des Davies. Tel Peterborough 63141. See community centres and associations for full list of community centres.

Education

Schools, colleges, teachers' centres etc are listed separately under "Education".
Chief education officer for Cambridgeshire: Mr G H Morris, Shire Hall, Cambridge. Tel 358811. Peterborough Area Education office: Touthill Close, Peterborough. Tel 52481.

Engineers' Department

City Engineer and controller of works: Mr O C Anderson, 24 Church Street, Peterborough. Tel 63141.

This department is responsible for administering all the city council's engineering and maintenance services, which include civil engineering and design, contract services on highway projects, main drainage and recreational facilities, heating, mechanical, electrical and structural design and services, traffic management and highways and main drainage, parks, recreation grounds, cemeteries and crematoriums, refuse collection and street lighting.

Environmental Health

Chief Environmental Health Officer: Mr K R Enderby, Equity and Law House, 19 Priestgate, Peterborough. Tel 63141.
Responsibilities include housing inspections, slum clearance and redevelopment, co-ordination of general improvement areas and improvement and home insulation grants, inspection of caravan sites and management of travellers' sites. Health and safety at work, clean air, noise abatement, nuisance control, food and food shop inspection, food hygiene education, notifiable infectious diseases and pest control.

Fire and Rescue

Cambridgeshire fire and rescue service provides a 24-hour cover for the county. In emergency, dial 999 and ask for the fire service.
County headquarters: Hinchingbrooke Cottage, Brampton Road, Huntingdon. Tel: Huntingdon 54651. Divisional fire safety officer: Dogsthorpe Road fire station, Peterborough. Tel 54081.

Police

Chief Constable: I H Kane, Police Headquarters, Hinchingbrooke Park, Huntingdon, Cambs. Tel Huntingdon 56111.
Peterborough police division is one of the areas into which the Cambridgeshire Constabulary is divided. Divisional headquarters are at Thorpe Wood police station, Thorpe Wood, Peterborough. Tel 63232.

Social Services

The social services function for the whole county is administered by the director. **Mr A F Jones, at Shire Hall, Cambridge. Tel 358811.** Almost all services are provided locally through the **Divisional Social Services Officer, Miss M P Foster, at Touthill Close, City Road, Peterborough. Tel 52481.**
This department covers children in difficulty with their families, a wide

range of special services for handicapped people, advice and help for parents of the mentally handicapped, advice and guidance for families experiencing mental illness, the home help service, a special laundry service for the elderly, meals-on-wheels, day care for the aged and sheltered workshops for the disabled.

Trading Standards

Chief Trading Standards officer: Mr M W Shipley, Hinchinbrooke Cottage, Brampton Road, Huntingdon. Tel Huntingdon 57344.
The aim is to create a better environment for close liaison between commerce and the public. If you have a problem relating to the inspection or testing of weighing or measuring equipment, quality, quantity, price and description of goods, contact the **consumer protection department, St Peter's Road, Peterborough. Tel 51577.**

Treasurers

City treasurer: Mr J F White, Town Hall, Peterborough. Tel 63141.
The department is responsible for collecting the rates for the city and county councils as well as other amounts due to the city for mortgages, bills and fines. It also issues bus and rail passes, pays the council's bills (including rent allowances), deals with investments with the city council and rate rebates.
The cash office in Bridge Street is open Monday to Friday 9am–4pm and Saturdays 9am–11.30am.
County director of finance and administration: Mr J E Barton, Shire Hall, Cambridge. Tel 358811.

Housing

Housing Officer: Mr B B Pryor, 10 Queen Street, Peterborough. Tel 63141.
This department manages and lets all the Peterborough City Council houses.

Information Centre

The City Council has an information centre in the Town Hall in Bridge Street. The staff gives information on a wide variety of subjects, including local government, clubs and associations, events, places to visit etc, as well as being a National Tourist Information Centre. Tel Peterborough 63141.

Land and Buildings

Director: Mr I M Purdy, Shire Hall, Cambridge. Tel 358811.

Legal and administration

Legal and administration officer: Mr M E Pearson, Town Hall, Peterborough. Tel 63141.
Deals with litigation and property transactions and as the city council's official secretary, prepares agendas and minutes for council and committee meetings and arranges for the implementation of decisions.
Estates manager and valuer: Mr I D G Wilson, Town Hall, Peterborough. Tel 63141.

Leisure and amenities

Leisure and amenities officer: Mr D G Constant, Town Hall, Peterborough. Tel 63141.
This department provides a wide range of leisure facilities for Peterborough. These include outdoor recreation and landscape design, indoor recreation, the city museum and art gallery (for details see under "The Arts"), the city council lottery. Responsibilities also include planning, design, management and maintenance of parks, commons, verges, amenity open spaces, recreation grounds, playgrounds, dual use areas, recreational sport, water related parks, riverside amenities, reclamation, housing estate amenity areas and managing the city's allotments. Also under this heading are sports centres and swimming pools (see under "Sport").
Outdoor recreation and landscape officer: Mr G Latham. Tel Peterborough 234018.

Libraries

Headquarters: Central Library, Broadway, Peterborough. Tel 48343.
See main heading "Libraries" for a full list.

Planning

City planning officer: Mr M S Pickering, 24 Church Street, Peterborough. Tel 63141.
This department deals with the use of land, control of building design and construction, and conservation of the environment, including preservation of trees and historic buildings. Most new buildings, including home extensions, require planning permission. Check first with a planning officer at the above address.
County director of planning and research: Mr R Brown, Shire Hall, Cambridge. Tel 358811.

This local information section was compiled with the help of . . .

PETERBOROUGH INFORMATION GROUP

Figure 12 The EMAP Trade Spotter Plus *directory*

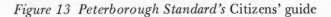

Figure 13 Peterborough Standard's Citizens' guide

those who others naturally go to for information. Try to identify such people and enlist their help, possibly by offering something in return. Bartering is a time-honoured system! Direct contact with individuals in other information services and organizations is often a better way of eliciting information than impersonal methods and also paves the way for further co-operation. Pay regular visits to such centres.

vi *Scanning newspapers, magazines, newsletters, etc* can turn up details of new organizations; changes of personnel, premises or hours of opening; new services introduced; and highlight problem areas where information may be needed.

vii *Other documents*, including council minutes and agendas, planning regulations, annual reports (ask to be put on mailing list for these), leaflets, and manifestos.

viii *Media publicity* Local press and radio may be prepared to put out a call for organizations to contact your service without charge. If not, then consider inserting an advert or, where there is a local directory produced, have a tear-out slip included for organizations to fill in and return to you.

As a result of these various methods, an amount of raw information will have been obtained which may be of use to your information service. How accurate, up-to-date, and complete the data is will depend very much on the reliability of its source. In most cases, unless you have every confidence in the source, the information will have to be checked before it is entered in a more permanent form in your resource file. So at this stage simply record it onto say a scrap 5in × 3in card and put it into a temporary file.

The information you have obtained will be of several different kinds but the most common will probably be that relating to organizations, clubs and societies. This is the most difficult type of information to collect since it is ever changing and therefore unrelenting effort will be required even to achieve reasonable completeness or accuracy — one hundred per cent will be impossible. However, with a good system for collecting and up-dating the information, you should be able to build up and maintain an acceptable file. A lot of the staff time will be needed to carry out this work, so first of all investigate whether there are other local information services that need this type of information and would be willing to help in its collection. It may be possible to collect the information through an umbrella group where the work can be farmed out so that it is not too great a burden on any one organization. Alternatively, a joint approach can be made on behalf of a number of organizations, as in the example shown here (Fig 14). This questionnaire is mailed out by a local newspaper, which needs the information for producing an area directory (see Fig 12), and when returned it is also passed on to four other services, the public library, the city information desk, the Citizens Advice Bureau and the Council for Voluntary Service.

Ideally the most effective way to collect information of this kind is to pay a personal visit to each organization or service, but rarely will that be possible without extensive staff resources or a very small community. The cheapest and quickest way to collect this information is by telephoning but this is only practicable given a reasonably small number to contact, say up to fifty. Prepare a standard list of questions to ask over the telephone so that entries in the Resources File are in a standard form. If visits and telephoning are ruled out, then the information can be collected initially by postal questionnaire with a request for up-to-date information sent at least once a year and also when it is known from other sources that changes have taken place. A covering letter should be sent with the questionnaire or up-date request, explaining why the information is needed and asking for co-operation. Also, include a stamped addressed envelope for return of the form, if it can be afforded, as this will significantly increase the response rate. Separate forms will be required to collect different kinds of information. The following is a suggested list of headings which you might consider including on forms for collecting information on two of the most common types of organization.

Clubs and societies
   (a)   *Name*: the name by which the club is best known plus the full name if different. Indication of relationship to larger body, ie branch, regiment, lodge, etc.

(b) *Secretary's name, address and telephone number* or a similar person if the organization has no secretary.
(c) *Place, day and time of meetings.*
(d) *Purpose of organization* if not self-evident from name.

Reply to: A. J. Bunch, BA, ALA, Central Library, Broadway, Peterborough, PE1 1RX. Tel. 48343 Ext. 25

Dear Secretary/Chairperson,

INFORMATION ON LOCAL CLUBS AND SOCIETIES

We are updating our files on local clubs and societies. I understand that you are or have been concerned with ....
I would be grateful if you could complete the form below and return it to me as soon as possible. This information will be passed on to the Central Reference Library, the Town Hall Information Desk, the Citizens Advice Bureau and Peterborough Council for Voluntary Service. It will also appear in the next edition of the Evening Telegraph Trade Spotter Plus directory which is distributed free to over 70,000 homes in the Peterborough area.

Thank you for your help in ensuring the continued success of these information services.

Yours sincerely,

Chairman

C.	SH.
T.	

Full name of organisation ....

Secretary ....

Address ....

.... Tel: ....

Place of meeting ....

Day and time ....

Purpose of club (if name is not self-explanatory) ....

....

Subscription ....

Date of Annual General Meeting ....

If you are a new club or have changed your officers (chairman, treasurer, etc.) in the last year, could you please fill in the back of this form.

PCVS	CL	THID	CAB

Signed ....

Figure 14 Peterborough Information Group questionnaire

(e) *Eligibility*: any restrictions by age, sex, ethnic group, occupation, status (single, divorced, widowed) etc.

(f) *Subscription*: any charge to become a member or to attend meetings.

(g) *Annual General Meeting*: useful as an indication of when to send out up-date forms.

(h) *Other officers*: names, addresses, telephone numbers of treasurer, president, chairman, publicity officer, membership secretary, etc.

(i) *History of organization* including special events or persons associated with it.

(j) *Publications*: newsletter, diary, commemorative brochures, etc.

*Agencies and organizations providing a service**

(a) *Name*: popular name and full name, eg CHAT (Come Here and Talk), SHAC (Shelter Housing Action Centre, plus relationship to parent body where necessary.

(b) *Address*: street address and postal address. Post Office box number if used.

(c) *Telephone number*: include service number, administration number, after-hours or emergency numbers. Telex number and code.

(d) *Contact person*: personal name, title and address (if different from (b)).

(e) *Hours of opening*: days and times. Note if seasonal, eg holiday period, school terms.

(f) *Services provided*: ask what enquiries the service would like to have referred to them.

(g) *Eligibility*: age, income, sex, residency, status.

(h) *Application procedures*: walk-in, appointment or waiting list? What documents or papers need to be brought.

(i) *Cost*: fees? free? means tested? donations? Any facilities for payments to be spread over a period? Help available from local or central government, charities, etc?

(j) *Geographical area served*: neighbourhood, city, county, region, ad hoc area? No geographical restrictions.

*This list is adapted from one in Turick, Dorothy *Community information services in libraries*. (Library Journal, New York, 1978.) A shorter list appears in *Who knows?* (National Consumer Council, 1982).

(k) *Branch offices*: extension bureaux, mobiles, surgeries, etc. Include hours of opening, routes and times of stops.

(l) *Director*: administrator or executive director of the service; name and telephone or extension.

(m) *Volunteers*: does the service use volunteers and for what purposes?

(n) *Publications*: directories, handbooks, leaflets, annual report, etc.

(o) *Funding*: local government, Urban Aid, Manpower Services Commission, charitable grants, donations, etc.

(p) *Special facilities*: foreign languages spoken, access for disabled, photocopying service, escort, advocacy, etc.

(q) *Transportation*: how to get to the service if transportation is necessary, eg bus route numbers, underground line and station.

These two lists represent most of the facts that an information service might need to know about an organization or service. In practice, depending on the scope of your service, it may not be necessary to include all the headings in the questionnaire. It is a good idea to get the person filling in the questionnaire to sign it, that way the information service has some protection against claims of giving wrong information, a not uncommon occurrence, especially when the information is to be published.

There are other types of 'soft' information that your service may need to collect, such as halls for hire, places of worship, accommodation, What's On events, local industry. The procedure is much the same:

* Decide what information you need to know.
* Devise a standard format or list of questions to ask.
* Identify possible sources of information.
* Decide which method or methods to use to collect the information: telephone, personal visit, postal questionnaire, press advert, etc.

How to store 'soft' information

There are various methods that can be used for storing information:

i *A list* is easy and quick to consult, can be photocopied for clients to take away, but has very little flexibility for inserting and up-dating information.

ii *A strip-index* provides flexibility, can easily be photo-copied, available in various forms: large binders holding many pages, smaller folders containing just a few pages, address books, wall hung panels, rotunda units, etc. Strips available in several colours, which allows for a simple categorization, and various widths. Even so, they are limited as to the amount of information that can be contained on them. Not quite as convenient to insert new strips as the manufacturers claim.

iii *Cards* are by far the most commonly used system for storing information. They are infinitely flexible, easy to insert and up-date and can be sorted into any preferred order. The two most popular sizes are 5in × 3in, which are used mainly for indexes or temporary information waiting to be checked, and 8in × 5in, which are large enough to contain sufficient information about most organizations or services and to be pre-printed with a standard grid for recording the information. There are more superior types of card file available, such as Rondofile or Rotadex (see pp41-43) but these are rather expensive and use custom designed stationery, whereas with

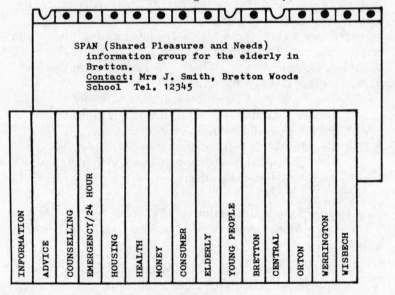

Figure 15 Edge-punched card filing system

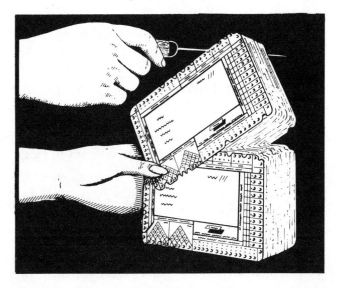

Figure 16 'Paramount' edge-punched cards

standard cards, if you are hard up, the reverse of scrap cards can always be used as an economy. Card files have two main disadvantages: they are not so easy to carry around and are not easily reproducible if someone wants a copy of a particular section eg sports clubs, churches, etc.

A primitive 'manual' computer can be devised using *edge-punched cards*. As you see from the illustration (Fig 15), the edge of each card is punched with a series of holes, each hole being allocated a category or subject which may relate to the type or interest of organizations, their location, clientele, etc. If an entry belongs to one or more of the categories, the piece of card between the hole and the edge of the card is cut away. Cards are usually filed alphabetically, then if the cards relating to a particular category or categories are required, rods or knitting needles are inserted into the appropriate holes. When the cards are lifted up, those remaining will be the ones required. A master card will be necessary for reference. You can, of course, carry the holes down both sides of the card for even more detailed categorization.

Cards selected have to be refiled each time. Edge-punched cards can be obtained from The Copeland-Chatterson Co. Ltd, Claire House, Bridge Street, Leatherhead, Surrey KT22 8HY. (Fig 16)

iv *Loose-leaf binders* with one sheet for each entry, sometimes called 'sheaf' binders, have a similar flexibility to cards. They are slightly slower to add to and amend but more portable. Suited best for alphabetical arrangements as they are difficult to guide.

v *Microcomputers* now have the capacity to handle the file needs of all but the very largest information services, as well as providing facilities for accessing videotext systems, like Prestel, and on-line information services. Information stored on microcomputers can be accessed by any number of predetermined variables — name, location, fields of interest, clientele, etc — and, with an add-on unit, this information can be printed out to satisfy one-off demands or to provide a master for printing. Micros may still be beyond the means of information services with limited funding, but the price of them continues to fall. It will not be too long before they become a recognized feature of most information services. An excellent guide to the capabilities and use of computers in information and advice work is *Computer benefits?: guidelines for local information and advice centres* by Pennie Ottley and Elaine Kempson (National Consumer Council, 1982).

Filing system
Whichever method is chosen for physically storing the information, except for that by microcomputer, it will be necessary to decide the best way of arranging entries so that the information can be retrieved swiftly and accurately. In order to ensure that the total resources of your information service are used to the full when answering an enquiry, it will help if the system used to organize the Resources File can be integrated with that for the vertical file and the bookstock. This point needs to be born in mind now, though it will be dealt with later under the subject file and classification.

The bulk of the Resources File will comprise 'soft' information which you have collected about organizations, clubs, societies and firms and, to a lesser extent, about individuals (eg doctors, tax consultants, Justices of the Peace) plus items of 'hard' information not available or conveniently available in printed form. There are several ways in which you might want to retrieve this information. Taking the example used to illustrate the edge-punched card on page 74, the information could be sought under the name of the organization (Shared Pleasures and Needs or SPAN), under the subject ie area of interest or clientele (the elderly), under the type of service (information group) or under the place (Bretton). In practice, the 'type of service' approach is rarely needed and is very similar to 'subject', so they will be treated together.

i *Organizations file*
The master file for the whole system will usually be an alphabetically arranged sequence of entries by name of organization. It is generally recommended that the full, official name of the organization is used, with references from other forms of the name. In practice, it doesn't really matter as long as there are references from the alternatives to whichever form is chosen. It could be argued that the popular version of a name is the one under which most people are likely to seek it first, so it would save time to file the main entry there, rather than a possibly lesser known official name.

Where many of the organizations all begin with the same word (a place name, for example), you may prefer to invert the heading eg ROSE SOCIETY, BLANKVILLE. Some people frown on inverted headings but they can be a useful way of introducing a kind of subject arrangement into what is basically a name file, eg

BLIND, ROYAL NATIONAL INSTITUTE FOR THE — Blankville Branch
BLIND, SUNSHINE CLUB FOR THE
BLIND, TALKING NEWSPAPER FOR THE

You will need to refer from the uninverted form of the name, eg

SUNSHINE CLUB FOR THE BLIND
see BLIND, SUNSHINE CLUB FOR THE

This only works, of course, for those organizations whose names indicate their sphere of activities.

In addition to details of organizations, each entry in the master file may also contain certain 'house-keeping' details relating to the maintenance of all the information files (see p81) plus references to appropriate headings in the subject file, where relevant information can be found, and a classification number (see p90).

ii *Subject file*

Most enquiries received by an information service are likely to be about the need for a service or activity or how to solve a problem, rather than for a specific named organization. So the information you have collected about organizations, services and individuals will need to be accessible also by the services and activities they provide. There are two ways this can be achieved, either using a subject index or having a subject file of organizations. In both, you will need to choose or adopt a set of subject headings which will adequately describe the information on file or elsewhere in the system and the interests of your clientele. You may not need to compile such a list yourself, there are a number of 'thesaurii' (lists of preferred terms, unpreferred terms, greater and smaller terms) covering particular subject areas eg *Getting started 5: Subject headings — the Help for Health thesaurus of indexing terms*, compiled by Robert Gann. (Wessex Regional Library & Information Service, 1982).

If you are compiling your own list of subject headings, choose terms that are in common use by your clientele, especially if they will be consulting the files themselves, rather than the 'official' term eg OUT OF WORK or ON THE DOLE instead of REDUNDANT. Always refer, however, from alternatives not used to the chosen term.

* A *subject index* is rather like the index to a book. It is an alphabetically arranged file of subject heading cards on which reference is made to where

information on that subject can be found. The cards themselves do not contain information. The subject index can contain references to organizations, individuals and other supplementary material, such as pamphlets, periodical articles, audio-visual material, books, etc. (See Fig 17)

* A *subject file of organizations* consists of an alphabetically arranged set of subject heading cards behind which are filed copies of the organization cards appropriate to that heading, plus cards containing items of 'hard' information.

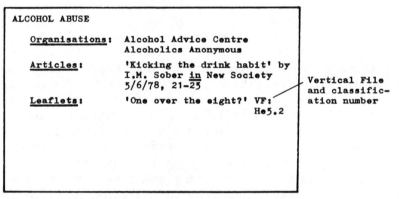

Figure 17 Subject index card

iii *Place file*

Where an information service covers a number of self-contained towns, villages or neighbourhoods, each having a similar range of organizations, it may be helpful to have a file that can be accessed by place. There are a number of options. You could sort the organizations file initially by place, especially if it contains few organizations whose responsibilities extend to the whole area covered by your service.

Alternatively, if most of the organizations are prefixed with the name of the place (eg EXVILLE ATHLETIC CLUB, EXVILLE DRAMATIC SOCIETY), the alphabetically arranged master file will automatically bring together those from the same location, provided you haven't inverted headings. Some arrangements will have to be made for organ-

izations which do not conform to the pattern, either
because the place name does not feature at the beginning or because it is not contained in the name of
the organization at all. In which case, an additional
card can be made out with either an inverted heading,
eg EXVILLE, ROTARY CLUB OF or the place name
can be prefixed eg EXVILLE – 20/30 CLUB.

The third option is to have a separate file of
organization cards arranged initially by place and
then alphabetically by name of organization or by
subject.

Filing alphabetically

Filing alphabetically is not quite as simple as ABC as any
librarian will tell you. There are two recognized methods,
known as 'Word by Word' and 'Letter by Letter'. In word by
word, entries are initially sorted by the first word in the
heading, then, headings that begin with the same word are
sorted by the second word and so on. Another way to describe this method, which may be helpful, is to treat spaces
between words in a heading as an imaginary letter coming
before 'a' in the alphabet, then sort 'letter by letter'.

Letter by letter you simply ignore any spaces in
the heading and sort one letter at a time from left to right.
Here is how a small group of headings would look sorted by
the two methods:

Word by Word	*Letter by Letter*
DO SOMETHING! BOYS CLUB	'DOG AND BONE' DARTS TEAM
'DOG AND BONE' DARTS TEAM	DOGSBURY RESIDENTS' ASSOCIATION
DOG SNIFFERS ANONY-MOUS	DOGS HOMES
DOGS HOMES	DOG SNIFFERS ANONY-MOUS
DOGSBURY RESIDENTS' ASSOCIATION	DO SOMETHING! BOYS CLUB

There are several other niceties to do with filing alphabetically but I need only mention here that hyphens are treated as
spaces in 'Word by Word' sorting and numerals are spelt out as
said. So that 1900 (the year) is NINETEEN HUNDRED and
1900 (the quantity) is ONE THOUSAND, NINE HUNDRED.

File housekeeping

In addition to the information needed to answer enquiries, there are other items of information to do with the maintenance of the file, which may usefully be included on each entry, such as:

* The date the information was obtained or last updated, which will indicate not only the degree of reliability to be placed on it but also when to update (see below);
* the date a questionnaire or update letter was sent — a check for chasing up non-returned forms;
* additional contacts or other information which does not fit onto the main part of the form;
* subject headings used in the subject file;
* place headings used in the place file, if not obvious from the name of the organization;
* feedback — comments from users of services;
* 'tracings', ie a list of other cards that refer to that entry, so that they can be traced and amended if subsequently it is altered or withdrawn.

The amount of this housekeeping information you need to include will depend on how sophisticated you need your file to be. The bigger the information service and the larger the file, then the more likely it is that you will need to introduce a systematic procedure for processing information. In which case the housekeeping information will need to go on the reverse of each entry, using a standard grid like the one illustrated here (Fig 18). For a small information service, it may be quite adequate just to note the date when the information was collected.

Updating

By its very nature the information contained in a Resources File will be changing continually. Hours of opening, meeting places, officers, membership fees, subscriptions, charges, etc are all susceptible to frequent changes. Therefore, it is important to have a system for regularly updating each entry in the file. There are several ways of achieving this, each having its own particular advantages or disadvantages but, whatever method you use, it must be regular and ongoing.

Interim updating

All the entries in the organizations file should be checked to see if they are up-to-date at least once a year. In between

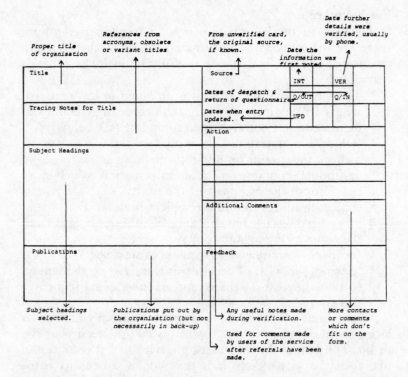

Figure 18 Tracings for file maintenance (From: Establishing a local community information service. Part 1: Guidelines for development and maintenance *by Anne L Keehan and Catherine Riatti. Library Board of Western Australia, 1982, 42)*

times, however, new information will be brought to the attention of your service by various means, including word of mouth, newspaper reports, organization newsletters, company reports and even, on rare occasions, by direct contact from the organization itself. If the source of the information is reliable, it can be substituted for the out of date information in the file but, if not, it should be noted and a further check made to verify its accuracy. A simple way to add new information to an existing card is to type or write it onto self-adhesive labels or slips (obtainable at most stationers) which can be stuck over the original information. Even though an entry has been updated in between times, it should still be checked formally once a year.

Annual updating

Most clubs, societies or organizations, if they are going to change their officers, generally do it once a year at an Annual General Meeting (AGM). So updating your information file at least annually should ensure that it keeps reasonably up-to-date with these changes. Of course, changes do occur in between AGMs and, if an information service feels it is necessary and has the staff resources, it is obviously better to check the file at shorter intervals, but most services, I'm sure, will probably be hard pressed to keep to an annual update.

AGMs are held at various times during the year, so try to avoid updating all the file at one set time, even if this is more convenient. In fact, in terms of work load, it is probably better to spread the updating throughout the year rather than have it all to do at once. By asking organizations to indicate on the initial questionnaire the approximate date of their AGM, it is possible to indicate on each entry in the file, by using an appropriate symbol such as a coloured dot, a letter or a card tag, when the information is due for updating.

All the cards falling due in a particular month are withdrawn from the file and either a new questionnaire is sent or, better still, a copy of the entry in the file, together with a covering letter is sent to the organization asking them to return it, indicating any changes. It is best if this is sent to organization secretaries just before their AGM so that, if there is a change of secretary, the form can be passed on to the new officer for return with the updated information.

·An alternative to sending out a copy of the entry is to 'phone each organization, but this is time consuming and costly and only feasible if the number of organizations to contact is fairly small.

Avoid sending out updates at times when people are likely to be away, such as during the summer holidays. There are certain times when it is more appropriate to update other kinds of information, eg social security benefit rates which usually change in April and September, adult education classes or school, college and university courses which change termly. Where an organization does not hold an AGM, simply update twelve months after the original information was received.

When an updated form is received it should be checked to see if the subject or place headings still apply. Any changes are either noted on the master card or a new card is made out to replace those in the subject or place files.

Supplementary information

Many organizations produce printed matter in the course of their work or activities. The most common types of material are directories or address lists of members (individuals or constituent groups), newsletters, events sheets or cards, annual reports, constitutions, posters, funding appeals, campaigning literature, advertising brochures, balance sheets, and commemorative booklets (anniversaries, etc). All this material is potentially useful as back up information to the Resources File but there is no sure way of obtaining it. When sending out the original questionnaire to organizations, you can ask to be put on their mailing list for this type of material, but such a request may prove too costly for an organization that operates on a shoestring. Then, regular receipt of material will depend very much on the enthusiasm or efficiency of the secretary of an organization, especially for things like newsletters. You could, of course, offer to pay for material to be sent, if your organization can afford it. The desirability of paying must be judged by the value of the publication to you.

When material arrives, it should be dated, so that you know roughly how old it is, and carefully filed for future use. The simplest method is to have an envelope or folder for each organization. Write on the outside of the envelope the name of the organization as used in your Resources File and arrange envelopes alphabetically in boxes or vertical file. You could also add to this file any cuttings from newspapers or magazines about organizations. The file should be checked regularly, at least once a year, and any out-of-date material withdrawn. When writing to organizations for updated information for the file, ask them also for any new literature.

Before throwing away the withdrawn material, check to see it it would be of use to some other organization or section of your service which collects material on local history.

Hard information

As well as the Resources File and its supplementary material, most information services will need a certain amount of 'hard' information to answer enquiries. Short, unrecorded or inadequately recorded items of 'hard' information, we have already seen, can be incorporated into the Resources File. However, the majority of hard information will usually be found in one or more of the vast range of print forms, starting from locally produced free broadsheets to multi-volumed loose-leaf reference works costing the earth. Within the scope of this book, it is not possible to go into detail about the sources of this material, since it will vary considerably according to the type and subject range of the service you are operating. Instead, I will simply reproduce a framework for collecting such material that originally was devised by Grainne Morby (Community Information Project) with some additions of my own:

1 *Distinguish between subject areas*, in other words identify the main topics into which the subject scope of your information service naturally divides. I will take, as an example, throughout this framework an information service whose area of interest is housing. It is sometimes useful to apply a consistent criteria when dividing up a subject, though obviously this would not be so easy for an information service whose scope is as broad as say the term 'community information'. But taking housing as our example, you could decide to divide it by type of accommodation eg owner-occupied, private-rented, council rented, New Town, institutional accommodation, tied accommodation, mobile homes, etc. In most cases you would probably need an additional general or miscellaneous category for subjects that cut across all or more than one category. In the case of housing this might be 'squatting' or 'homelessness'.

2 *What are the information needs of specific client-groups within the subject areas?* Since the material you want to collect will usually be written to meet a particular need or needs, it is advisable to collect information around those needs rather than a theoretical framework. The kind of broad client groups that might be identified in the field of housing are landlords, tenants, owner-occupiers, squatters, transients, elderly people, disabled. Then, one could identify client groups who share a common problem or need associated with their particular type of accommodation, such as eviction, dampness, house repair, renovation, harassment by landlord, mortgages, rent arrears, planning permission, etc.

Once these subject areas and client needs have been identified, it should give you clearer guidelines when you come to select material for your information service from the various sources referred to in the next part of the framework.

3 *Print sources*
  (a) Official
      i National
          — pre-legislation: political party manifestos and policy documents, speeches by Ministers, the Queen's Speech at opening of Parliament
          — legislation: Bills, Hansard reports of debates in both Houses of Parliament, Acts, Statutory Instruments
          — guidance to local statutory bodies: circulars and letters from Ministers, guidance notes, reports of Inspectors
          — reference books: collections of legislation eg *Statutes in force, Legal aid handbook*, the 'Brown book' etc.
          — periodicals from government departments and quangos*, eg *Department of Employment gazette, British business, The Clapham omnibus*
          — guidance to public ie leaflets, posters, audio-visual packs, from government departments and quangos.
      ii Regional
          — public utilities: gas, electricity, water, solid fuel boards, Small Firms Information Service, regional health authorities, regional tourist boards
          — consumer watchdog bodies: Post Office Users' National Council (POUNC), gas and electricity consultative committees.
      iii Local
          — local authority policies and decisions: agendas, minutes, standing orders, byelaws and regulations
          — guidance to public: handbooks, leaflets, etc from local authorities, area and district health

*Quasi-Autonomous National Government Organizations eg Equal Opportunities Commission, National Consumer Council, British Tourist Authority.

authorities, water divisions, Community Health
Councils, local offices of government agencies
(b) Non-official
   i National
      — reference books from commercial publishers
      — voluntary organizations
      — pressure groups, self-help groups
      — 'umbrella' organizations eg National Council for
      Voluntary Organizations, Federation of Inde-
      pendent Advice Centres, etc
      — professional bodies eg The Law Society
      — trade associations eg National Association of
      Retail Furnishers
      — educational bodies eg National Extension College
      — trade unions
      — the media
      — practitioners in the field who publish.
   ii Local
      — claimants' unions
      — law centres, other specialist advice centres
      — neighbourhood and generalist advice centres,
      resource centres
      — pressure groups, action centres
      — voluntary organizations
   iii New technology
      — videotext systems: Prestel, teletext, private
      viewdata
      — on-line computer service
      — anything else that may come along in the future.
      Look out for videodiscs, cable television, etc.

Obtaining publications and other printed material
Once the material you require has been identified, you will
need to obtain it. Some material will be priced, in which
case an order must be placed, and some will be free.

(a) *Priced publications*
The procedrue for ordering priced publications from official
and non-official bodies varies considerably. Some have their
own order forms which must be used (eg HMSO), some will
accept official orders, others operate a standing order service
or insist on money with order. Whatever the method, it is

important to keep a record of what has been placed on order
and from whom to avoid duplication of titles and as a check
on supply. So, for each title make out an order card — this
can be either a scrap 5in × 3in card or one specially printed
with a standard grid. The kind of information that needs to
be recorded on the card is:

* title of the publication — more important than author
  for this kind of material, since authorship is often
  unclear.
* author — might be an individual or an organization
* price, date of publication and frequency, if a periodical
* supplier — this may be a bookseller, library supplier
  or the address of the producing body.
* date of order.
* source of information.
* location if you are ordering for more than one centre.

You may find it helpful to use the order cards later as the
basis of a catalogue of the publications in your information
centre. In which case, leave space at the top of the card for
either a subject heading, classification number or filing code.

After an order has been raised and sent to the supplier,
the order cards are filed, preferably by title, in one alphabetical sequence known as the 'order file'. When a publication
arrives, the order card is removed from the file and accom-
panies it to the next stage if it is to be used later as the catalogue card. If not, you may find it useful to file the order
card in a 'publications received' file, until such time as the
publication is permanently recorded in the system, after
which it can be thrown away.

(b) *Periodicals*
Publications which arrive at regular intervals — weekly,
fortnightly, monthly and quarterly — will not require an
order card but you will need to keep a record of what is
received. This should include the following items of information:

* title of periodical
* frequency
* supplier
* when subscription is due for payment
* a grid to record receipt of each issue
* instructions for disposal of back copies

(c) *Free material*

This can vary from quite substantial booklets to leaflets, posters and bookmarks and may be required singly or in bulk. Since this is likely to be a frequent type of request, it is quicker and simpler to duplicate a standard letter to send to organizations, with space left to fill in address, title of item, format (leaflet, booklet, poster, etc) and number of copies required. It is advisable to keep some record of what is requested, if only as a check on whether it has been received or not. Where you are ordering in bulk for several centres, a card or slip such as that shown here (Fig 19) can serve as a request slip for each centre, the order record and, when copies are received, the distribution record. File cards for free materials either in the order file or in a separate section.

LEAFLET REQUEST SLIP		DATE ORDERED			
TITLE OF LEAFLET					
		NUMBER OF COPIES			
NAME AND ADDRESS OF SUPPLIER		DISTRIBUTION			
		C		Wh	
		B		Wi	
		M		Y	
CENTRE	NUMBER REQUIRED	O			
		We			

Figure 19 Leaflet request slip or card

Organizing 'hard' information

We have already seen that 'hard' information can be found in a great variety of published forms. For the benefit of organizing it, the following categories can be identified:

(a) *Material in book form* for use by clientele or information workers will be best arranged on shelves in the broad subject groups identified when acquiring the material (see p85) or according to a classification scheme (see below).

(b) *Ephemeral material for use by information workers* can be stored in a vertical file using the same headings as those in the subject sequence of the Resources File, though probably with more sub-divisions, or using a classification scheme. Alternatively, the material can be kept in file boxes on shelves using broad subject headings.

(c) *Ephemeral material for use by clientele on the premises* may be best stored in file boxes on the shelves according to the method used for arranging the books. Vertical files are not recommended for public use as they are too much of a deterrent. Another system is to gather ephemeral materials on particular topics together in packs (see p117) and to display them face outwards on sloping shelves for maximum impact.

(d) *Ephemeral material for the public to take away* can be displayed in special leaflet dispensers, on a sloping surface or on tables. Ideally, they should be displayed in broad subject groups but this is rarely possible.

Classification

It is not my intention to go into any great detail about the classification of materials in information centres. For most small information services, it will be quite adequate to arrange material by broad subject groups sub-divided according to the form in which the clientele's needs and problems are presented. For ease of labelling vertical files, book spines and boxes, a simple notation can be used based on the initial letter or letters of subjects. Taking the earlier example of housing, a possible range of subjects and notations might be:

A — Agricultural accommodation	Re — Rented accommodation
H — Homelessness	ReC — Council housing
I — Institutional accommodation	ReN — New Town housing
	ReP — Private rented
M — Mobile homes	S — Squatting
O — Owner-occupied	
Ra — Rates	

Numerals can be introduced for more detailed sub-divisions,

eg, O_1 — Buying and selling a house; O_2 — Home insurance; O_3 — Planning applications, etc. An effective method that can be used where you have only a small number of broad subjects groups (no more than ten and preferably less) is colour coding. Allocate a colour to each subject and stick an appropriate coloured label or tape on the spine of each book or file box. Colour coding can be used in conjunction with notation to provide more detailed sub-division of a subject.

When an information service grows to a size where broad subject grouping is not adequate to contain all the material and allow efficient retrieval, then it may be time to consider using a classification scheme. Two choices are open to you, either using or adapting a ready-made scheme or constructing your own. There are a number of general classification schemes used in libraries, of which the most well-known is the Dewey Decimal Classification. These schemes have been constructed to organize the whole of knowledge and subjects are usually arranged on philosophical or logical principles. Consequently, they may not be sufficiently detailed or treat subjects in the way your clientele express their information needs. Most schemes have a certain degree of flexibility and it might be possible to adapt them. There are other classification schemes covering narrower subject fields of which the following are perhaps worth a mention:

Gann, Robert *Getting started 6: a classification scheme for patient information.* Wessex Regional Library & Information Service, 1982.

Aitchison, Jean *Thesaurus on youth.* National Youth Bureau, 1981 — contains an integrated classification and thesaurus.

The National Association of Citizens' Advice Bureaux (NACAB) has its own scheme for arranging materials on the broad area of community information, but it hardly merits the description of a 'classification scheme' and in recent years has been proving inadequate for the task. A new, properly constructed classification scheme is being developed for NACAB and should be available some time in the near future.

Constructing your own classification scheme is not a task to be entered into lightly and it is certainly not within the scope of this basic guide to describe how to go about it. If you would like to have a go, I can refer you to a book produced by the Community Information Service of the

Northern Ireland Council of Social Service called *Designing a community information system* (NICSS, 2 Annadale Avenue, Belfast BT7, 1980, £1.00) which describes, step by step, the process they went through in constructing a classification scheme to meet their own needs. The scheme is also reproduced in the book.

The parts of this chapter on organizing information have of necessity been kept as simple and as brief as possible. A more detailed approach to the subject will be found in another title in this series called *The basics of organizing information* by Chris Turner (Library Association Publishing, 1984).

Chapter Four

Giving out information

Once you have built up the information base of your service, then the next step is to consider how that information is to be made available to potential users of the service. There are a number of possibilities:
* face to face contact with clients
* by telephone
* postal requests
* by display
* selective dissemination of information (SDI)
* indirectly to clients through deposit files
* through publications
    − to other information workers, professionals or groups
    − to clientele
* information packs
* through the media.

Not every information service will want or need to adopt all these methods. It may be that, when the assessment of need for your service was carried out (see Chapter 1), there was a clear indication of which method of dissemination would be most appropriate. Nevertheless, it is worth exploring other means, since the effectiveness of your information service should be constantly under review and it may be that more people could be reached by adopting a new or different method of dissemination.

(a) *Face to face contact with clientele* This is the passive function, whereby an information service is located in a particular building or room and the clientele call in person to seek information for themselves or from the staff by enquiry at an information desk. It has the advantages that the most up-to-date information is available, provided the service has carried out its information gathering efficiently; the client can be interviewed to reveal exactly what information is required; and the help of a member of staff familiar with using the files is on hand to search out information, to make contact with services, or to suggest further possible courses of action.

Some disadvantages to having one defined location are that, unless it is well sited (in the High Street or shopping centre), it may be difficult to bring the service to the attention of potential users without a continual publicity campaign; it is expensive to operate in terms of the resources needed to staff the enquiry desk continually and to stay open outside normal office hours.

Dealing with people face to face requires a certain amount of skill but, above all, is the need to have a pleasant and approachable personality, a characteristic that is not so easily learnt. The following guidelines may be helpful in interviewing clients:

i   First of all, try to make the enquirer feel at ease, so that s/he is not afraid to ask questions or discuss a problem. It may seem a trivial enquiry to you but could be causing the client much anxiety.

ii Do not exhibit feelings of shock, horror, amusement, disbelief or repugnance at anything the client says. It is not part of your job to pass judgement on a client whose behaviour or ideas are contrary to the norms of society.

iii Listen to the whole query and don't start jumping to conclusions before the enquirer has finished. Listen 'actively' by asking appropriate questions to clarify what is specifically being asked, since most people tend to phrase their questions in general terms. What the client wants may not necessarily be what they need.

iv When you think you know what is being requested, state it in simple terms so that the enquirer can confirm that you are on the right track. I once spent ages looking through modern dance manuals to answer a request for information on 'how to jive' only to find, after proudly presenting a suitable book, that the enquirer had a speech impediment and really wanted to know 'how to djive a car'!

v   Try to identify with the enquirer's problem, at the same time remaining impartial and emotionally un-involved. That is probably an unattainable counsel of perfection but it is only a warning that sometimes people ask the impossible or want confirmation or support for a course of action when they are in the wrong. Even where a service sets out to be partial, it cannot support clients irrespective of whether they are right or wrong. It may be necessary at times to give information or advice that is contrary to the client's expectations.

vi   Before any information is given it should, wherever possible, be double checked to ensure that it is correct and, if reasonably brief, written down to give to the client.

vii   Where there are alternative courses of action, explain these to the client in simple terms and leave him or her to make the choice unless you are specifically offering an advice service.

viii   Never leave the client with a negative response even where you cannot answer the query. Suggest where else the client may go to find an answer, even making a telephone call, if necessary, to fix an appointment or make an introduction. If the enquiry needs further searching and is not urgent, take down the details on the standard request form (see p14) and offer to 'phone or write with the answer as soon as possible. Suggest that the enquirer calls back after a certain interval if they have not had a reply.

(b)   *By telephone* The facility to transmit information by telephone can be an advantage, especially where clientele have difficulty in reaching an information service because of its location or their own physical disabilities. Some people actually prefer the greater anonymity of the telephone. From the point of view of the service, the location of one that is based mainly or entirely on use by telephone is not so crucial. Staff can be occupied with other work in between calls and do not have to be tied to an enquiry desk, thus it may be possible to offer longer hours. With the additional use of an answer machine, a service is able to offer a twenty-four hour, seven days a week service. A conference 'phone facility enables three-way link-ups to be made and clients can be put in direct contact with a service that can help them.

However, telephones, in Britain at least, are still by no means universally available and public call-boxes, when they haven't been vandalized, are frequently inconvenient because of their location or continual use. Some people are deterred from using telephones because they experience difficulties in expressing themselves via this medium or the cost of making calls is a financial burden. This latter point can be overcome by operating a Freephone system or offering to ring the caller back as soon as contact is made if your organization can afford it.

Telephones are best suited for answering enquiries that are brief, clearly stated and uncomplicated. Time does not allow for lengthy interviewing of the client on the 'phone, nor is it possible to pick up those non-verbal signals which often help in assessing the true need of the client. Likewise, the client cannot see you — so make your voice welcoming. Here are some tips on answering the telephone based on the English Tourist Board's booklet *Can I help you?* (English Trouist Board, 1980).

i   Make sure you always have a supply of pencils and paper near the telephone and that the most used sources of information are readily to hand.

ii Answer the telephone promptly. You may think that letting it ring is a smart way of getting over the message that you are busy but it only annoys the caller who imagines that you are either drinking tea, filing your finger nails or having an interesting discussion about last night's television programme.

iii Never use "ello!' — it is too casual and, at this stage the caller is not certain that they have got through to the right service or not. Always say who you are (the service, not 'Joan 'ere') and offer to help.

iv If the caller gives their name always use it.

v   Do not smoke, eat, or drink when speaking on the 'phone, it impedes your speech.

vi Jot down the details of the query as it is given and

confirm with the caller the essence of their enquiry before answering.

vii If you have to ask the caller to wait or need to leave the telephone to look up information, explain what is happening and when returning, thank the caller for waiting.

viii If it is obvious from the start or after an initial search that the query may take some time to answer, offer to ring back the caller — *not* forgetting to take down their telephone number and name (if you haven't got it already). If the enquirer is ringing from a public call box, either ask them to 'phone back later or take down name and address and post the reply.

ix When answering a query by telephone, ask the caller to read back any crucial information such as amounts of money, telephone numbers, etc as a check that they have been taken down correctly.

x At the end of an enquiry, thank the person for calling. Be positive even if the reply is negative. It's better to say 'Sorry we haven't been able to help you on this occasion but thank you for calling and please get in touch again if you have any other queries' than 'Sorry, can't help you' — click.

(c) *By post* Requests for information by post do not as a rule figure very prominently in the work of an information service, but they are just as important. There is a temptation to assume that postal enquiries are less urgent than the client who is breathing down your neck or hanging on the end of a telephone and so can be dealt with whenever there is a spare moment — in other words, never! But this may not be the case and therefore such enquiries should be dealt with just as expeditiously as any other.

A fairly common type of postal enquiry from individuals, organizations and commercial concerns is that for a list of clubs and societies on a particular topic or in a particular area. It is obviously an advantage if you have a filing system which enables you to print out a section of the resources file on request. But failing that, you can either invite the requesting body to call in and examine your file or you can list the organizations yourself. This can be a very time-consuming process and if this kind of request is received

frequently, it may be worth considering having sections of
the file printed as leaflets or lists that can be sent off on
request (see also p104).

Where a postal request is likely to take a little time in
being answered, send off a pre-printed acknowledgement
slip on receipt of the enquiry, saying something like: 'Thank
you for your enquiry which is receiving our attention. We
will try to send you an answer as soon as possible.'

(d) *By display* People have an innate tendency to browse,
picking up information in a rather ad hoc, casual fashion. An
information service can take advantage of this by providing
well-sited, attractive and interesting displays for putting
over information to clients and passers-by. There are four
main aspects of display (i) noticeboards, (ii) thematic
displays, (iii) window display and (iv) outside display.

   i *Noticeboards.* A great deal of information is available
      in poster or broadsheet format. Some of it is free,
      some will come unsolicited and there are a few poster
      for which you have to pay. There are basically four
      types of poster:
      * the 'event' poster gives details of something that is
         to take place at a particular time;
      * the 'service' poster gives details of a service that is
         available — its opening hours, location, who is
         eligible, how to contact, etc — and is not, as a
         rule, restricted to a finite date;
      * the 'information' poster presents 'hard' information
         in an encapsulated form — benefit rates, changes in
         legislation, rights information, eligibility for grants,
         health education, etc;
      * the 'persuasive' poster endeavours to sell us a
         product, change our opinions, enlist our sympathy
         and support.
      The first three types of poster should not cause an
      information service any problems regarding the policy
      of whether to display or not, but the last category
      can require some problematical decisions. If your
      information service is part of a larger organization,
      then it would be helpful to have clear guidelines on
      what is or is not allowed to be displayed. Try to avoid
      the too simplistic approach of either displaying every-

thing or nothing at all. It is usual to rule out commercial advertising and, in some cases, 'political' posters. How you interpret what is 'political' is open to debate. Party debate. Party political posters would clearly come within the definition of 'political' but what about posters campaigning for or against issues which are subjects of political debate? An 'open door' policy may, in theory, sound fine but in practice it can throw up just as many problems, such as your right to refuse to display a poster which may not be in the public interest but does not necessarily contravene the law.

There is more to displaying posters or other notices than simply sticking in a few drawing pins. Here are a few points you might find useful:

* You can never (or rarely) have enough notice board space, so in planning an information service — think big!
* If you have several boards, categorize them eg coming events, sources of help, places to visit, etc.
* Don't overcrowd your noticeboards — posters should never be overlapping and obscuring each other. If you only have a limited space, change the posters regularly to give each one a chance.
* Arrange posters to look attractive — contrast posters of different shapes or colours to add interest. Move long-term posters around from time to time to give the impression of change.
* Check noticeboards every day to ensure that out)ut date posters are not left on display.

ii *Thematic displays* Displays devoted to a particular topic or theme, if well produced, can be a useful way of drawing attention to information that is available. The theme may (a) concern a problem area identified from an analysis of enquiries, (b) relate to a current change in legislation or benefit rates, (c) be aimed at improving public awareness of an issue of current concern, (d) draw attention to benefits, grants, services or rights that your clientele may not be aware of before, (e) canvass support for a cause, and (f) educate the public on personal matters eg health, finance, etc.

Use notice boards or, better still, free-standing boards, where you have space and can afford or get hold of them, to mount displays. There is some skill required in preparing materials and mounting an attractive display which there is not space to go into here. If you don't feel confident to do it yourself, find out if there is someone in your organization who has a flair for this kind of work and is willing to help.

There are a number of organizations, including government departments, which have displays that can be loaned free of charge or carriage paid one way.

iii *Window display* If your information service is fortunate enough to be housed in a building that has a large window at ground-level overlooking a thoroughfare, then this can be used to good effect in giving out information not only to users of your service but also to casual passers-by. Displays such as those described in the section above, placed in the window, would enable the information to reach beyond your own clientele and may even encourage increased use of the service. An external window can also be used for displaying essential information, such as addresses and telephone numbers of emergency services, hotel accommodation and camping sites, when your service is closed. Other types of information suitable for window display are small ads and job vacancies.

Small ads may seem trivial but they do fill an important information need in most communities and also have the added bonus of attracting people to look in your window and, perhaps, thereby become more aware of the information service and what it can offer. Don't set up a small ads service in direct competition with the little newsagent next door.

Job vacancies is a much appreciated service, particularly at times of high unemployment. Access to job centres is not always easy because of distance or cost of travel, so a locally based job vacancies board can provide a valuable service to the community. Either contact local firms, businesses, shops, etc and ask if they would be prepared to display their job vacancies in your window or ask your nearest Job Centre if they would send you job vacancy cards on a regular basis. If you can afford to do so, offer to contact firm or Job Centre on behalf of any client who is interested in a particular job advertised, to see if it is still vacant.

Plastic display holders for small ads or job vacancy cards can be obtained from Moons Strip Systems Ltd, 3 Eastfield Road, Burniham, Bucks.

iv *Outside display* As well as displaying information in your own centre, consider the possibilities of display in other buildings. Many organizations such as libraries, community centres, clinics, schools, local government offices, etc. whose doors are open to the public, are often prepared to accept the kind of displays referred to in section iii. above. It may be possible to circulate such displays around a number of centres and thus reach a much wider audience. Some commercial businesses, like banks and building societies, who rarely have anything interesting to show in their windows, encourage organizations to use these for displays.

With displays located on other people's premises, you will have to accept their right to reject all or part of your display if it is objectionable to them or not produced to a high enough standard. Find out first if the organization or business has a policy on what can or cannot be displayed and whether they have their own display equipment. For outside displays, other than simply posters to be pinned to a wall, you will need spare display boards that can be released for a length of time and the means to transport them. The display should be checked regularly to maintain stocks of any give-away leaflets, etc, to ensure the currency of the information, and to keep it in good repair.

Another possible outlet for information is community notice boards, which are usually located in prominent positions such as market squares, shopping malls, etc. They are most likely to be owned

by the local council but it is not unknown for councils
to assign the running of such boards to a local information centre. The sort of information best suited
for this type of board is directional (map of village,
town or neighbourhood and street index) showing
places of interest and sources of help (information
and advice centres, local government services) and
coming events.

(e)   *Selective dissemination of information (SDI)* This is a
rather forbidding term to describe a process for transmitting
information that many information services adopt quite
unconsciously without ever having heard of SDI, so don't
worry. It simply means taking note of the subject interests of
particular individuals or groups who use your service and
supplying them new information as it becomes available.
'Taking note' can be a fairly organized and formal system
involving the sending out of a questionnaire to discover user's
interests and maintaining a card file (usually arranged by
subject) of those interests but, more often than not, it is
something stored in the information worker's head ('I know
Joe Bloggs is interested in this, I'll send him a copy'). SDI is
most often used by services whose clientele are a closed
group — an organization or firm — rather than ones serving
the general public. Where generalist services operate SDI, it
will usually be for other information workers, community
workers, professionals or groups.

An SDI service can include regular scanning of new publications, journals, newspapers, press releases, annual reports,
balance sheets, product literature and other ephemeral material
or it may be rather unsystematic and random. Either way, it
is a useful service, particularly for those individuals, organizations or groups who need a supply of new information in
their area of interest but do not have the time, resources or
expertise to search it out. It is an excellent way to win
friends for your information service who in turn may be able
to help you on other occasions.

(f)   *Deposit files and collections* One solution to the problem
of having one fixed location from which to give out information is to duplicate your resources file or other material
and to deposit it at outlying centres. This would obviously
make it more accessible to a wider clientele but has the

disadvantages that (i) it is more difficult to keep several files or collections current, especially where you have to rely on someone else to do the updating, and (ii) staff, where they exist, need to be trained in using the file or collections, so that they can help clients.

Files using loose-leaf binders or strip indexes are easier to duplicate than card files. Looking to the future and a wider availability of microcomputers, then it is a fairly easy process to duplicate information files on floppy discs and locate them at remote centres or simply have a terminal there which can access one main computer file.

A good example of an information service that is dupli- cated and made widely available is that of the National Association of Citizens Advice Bureaux. This consists of a basic file covering 14 subject areas made up of specially prepared loose-leaf information sheets, together with leaflets, forms etc from statutory and non-statutory bodies, plus monthly updates. There are now two levels available — the full service, which requires the approval of the local CAB and Area Office to obtain it, and the mini-pack, contained in two loose-leaf binders. Details of both services can be obtained from NACAB, 110 Drury Lane, London WC2B 3HH.

(g) *Publications* These are one of the best means of making the information collected by your service more accessible to a wider range of people than you could ever hope to reach through a static service point. Well produced and attractive publications enhance the image of an information service and help to attract custom. The commitment of information to print inevitably attracts corrections, additions, etc which enable your service to maintain an even more accurate and up-to-date resources file.

Producing publications of reasonable quality can be costly both in time and money, although it pays to shop around for printers. Some community printers and resource centes offer services at virtually cost price of materials. Alternatively, explore the possibilities of joint publication with other organizations, obtaining a grant from an appropriate body who may have an interest in your publication, or using adver- tising to pay for all or part of the costs.

Once information is printed, it is static and, therefore, liable to date in a short space of time. When producing publications always consider your ability to sustain not only the one issue but also any future new editions which may be necessary, to distribute the finished copy, either as a one-off or regularly, or to handle sales. All these can be very time consuming. It is an acceptable strategy, of course, to publish one issue in the hopes that its value will be recognized and future issues attract funding. The frequency with which you need to update the publication should determine the format you choose, whether it should be loose-leaf or not, a leaflet or a booklet.

Publications may be aimed at basically two kinds of user: those whose work or status consists wholly or in part in informing others and those whom we might term your general clientele. They may be the public, a section of the public, or members of a particular organization or group. The major differences between the two in respect of publications will lie in the degree of detail and the way the information is presented.

How do you know what to publish?
* The kind of enquiries your information service receives will be one indicator. Frequent requests for the same type of information, eg places in the locality to visit, could be more quickly answered if a printed list or leaflet is available to give away.
* In collecting 'hard' information you may recognize a gap in the available literature that your information service could fill with an appropriate publication.
* Talk to other information and advice workers, they may have some ideas on what subjects there is a lack of information.
* Identify specific groups of user who have defined information needs, eg elderly people, the disabled, parents with children under five, school leavers, etc which might be met with a suitable publication.

Types of publication

1 *Lists*
These are the simplest forms of publication to compile, often arising out of repeated requests for the same kind of information, eg names and addresses of estate agents, firms offering specialized services; places to eat, etc. A list can be just a

single side of paper or several sheets stapled together. The arrangement is usually either straight alphabetical or alphabetical under subject or place headings, depending on the topic. Lists are given out in response to an enquiry, so do not require a great deal of creative design in their production. The use of an attractive pre-printed headed paper with the logo of your service, if you have one, its address and telephone number can make a humble list a little more attractive and helps to publicize the service (see Fig 20). Small numbers of lists can be run off on a photocopier; for longer runs use a stencil duplicator or an offset litho printer. If you do not have print facilities yourself, most towns of any size nowadays usually have at least one instant print shop where good quality copies can be obtained at a fairly reasonable price and quickly.

2 *Leaflets*

A leaflet in one respect is a kind of extrovert list; it goes out of its way to attract attention and encourage people to pick it up. This is the *information* type of leaflet, whose contents may be much the same as a list. The two other main types are the *educational* leaflet, whose objective is to improve the quality of life of those for whom it has been produced or, generally, to increase understanding of a particular subject, and the *campaigning* leaflet which sets out either to convert someone from one point of view to another, to gain sympathy and support for a cause, or to change a certain state of affairs for the better.

Thousands of leaflets are produced each year by all kinds of bodies. The quality of these leaflets varies from the extremely glossy and eye catching to the cheap and nasty. If you are going to enter this arena, then it is important to give as much attention to the design of your leaflet as to its contents, since it will have to compete for attention with commercial products. However, you don't have to be an artist or a designer to be able to produce an attractive leaflet. Look around at examples of commercially produced leaflets and copy ideas that appeal to you. Advertising can also be a source of abundant 'free' or non-attributable art to illustrate and add impact to your own leaflets. Other sources of material might include old engravings (particularly of the Victorian era), drawings of the great masters (Leonardo da Vinci,

Dürer, Michelangelo, etc) and instant art books,[1] but these can be a little expensive. Lettering in a wide variety of styles which can be rubbed onto artwork is available in large and small sheets from most stationers or your organization may well have invested in one of these instant lettering machines. Use cartoons, diagrams, graphs and photographs to liven up the text. Keep wording simple and short (pretend you are writing for the 'Daily Mirror'!). Standard sizes of leaflets

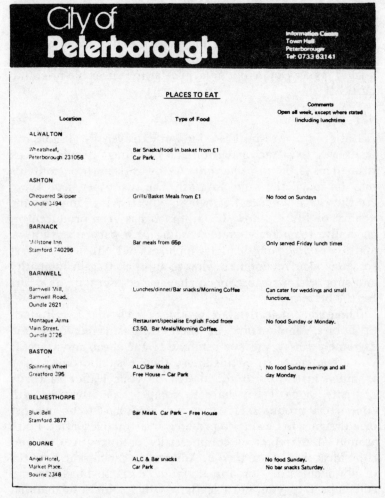

Figure 20 Peterborough Town Hall Information Centre's Places to eat *list*

A5 (149mm × 210mm) and 1/3A4 (99mm × 210mm), but experiment with unusual sizes based on standard sheets for added impact. Have enough copies printed to give a wide circulation and distribute them through as many outlets as possible, particularly those which attract large numbers of people. Investigate other means of distribution that might give you an even wider coverage, such as insertion in free community newspaper, included with council rate demand, or through organizations who regularly send out to a large mailing list.

3 Posters

The aim of a poster is to present a small amount of information with the maximum amount of impact so that 'he who runs may read'. Use posters to advertised events, to draw attention to a few sources of information or advice, or to point out eligibility for a service or benefit. Much of the advice given above about the design of leaflets applies equally to designing posters. The design of a poster should emphasize the information that you want to convey.

Don't make the poster too big as this may create problems for those who you might wish to display it, since most organizations do not have unlimited display space. A3 (298 × 420mm) is the most popular and useful size; A4 (210 × 298mm) is a little small to make a great deal of impact but may be more acceptable if you want organizations to display the poster for a long time. A one-off poster can be prepared by hand if you have someone artistically inclined, but for any quantity you will need to use either a printer or a good photocopying machine. Plain paper copiers are fairly common nowadays and some have the facility to reproduce up to A3 size. The better machines can reproduce copy in dense black, including photographs, drawings etc. Coloured paper can also be obtained for photocopying machines in a range of pastel shades. Some machines have the facility to reduce the original down to a smaller size and a few coming onto the market now can even enlarge. Another method of reproducing posters is by silk-screen, which is a kind of stencil process. Some community arts centres make silk screen facilities available to groups and will show you how to go about it.

Some useful tips on producing leaflets and posters can be found in the following books:

Fry, Alan *Layout and design*. Sunderland Community Press, 470 Hylton Road, Sunderland, 1981, 45p.
Zeitlyn, Jonathan *Print: how you can do it yourself*. 3rd ed rev. Inter-Action Inprint, 1980.

4 *Directories*

A directory is one of the most useful publications that an information service can produce. It may cover the whole of a community, be confined to the interests of a particular client group, or contain information about a certain type of organization, eg social welfare agencies or exporters. A directory plays an important role in community development by informing people about the services that exist and thus encouraging them to take a more active part in community life. It helps newcomers fit into the community and is a tool for those people to whom others turn for help and advice.

A directory will usually be based on the information service's resources file but reproduced in a format that is easy to understand and use. There are a number of decisions to make before you embark on producing a directory:

i *Who is it aimed at?* The general public, ie all households and businesses, sections of the public with special needs, community groups, community leaders, etc.

ii *How many copies will be required?* This will depend on whether you decide to distribute to everyone, in which case you need to obtain an estimate of your target group. If it is not feasible to give it such a wide distribution, then you must decide on how many copies it is realistically possible to produce within your budget.

iii *How much will it cost?* You will need to work out as accurately as possible what size the directory will be so that estimates can be obtained from printers. Allow for advertising space if you are using this method to finance the directory. Newspapers work on a formula of two thirds advertising to one third editorial (information) but they have greater overheads to contend with. Half-and-half or even less may be an acceptable proportion depending on whether the advertising is intended to cover the whole cost.

iv *How is it to be funded?* From your own budget? By special allocation from your parent body? Joint funding with other agencies? Grants from outside bodies? Advertising? Sales? Or a combination of several of these? There has been a lot of interest shown by newspapers in recent years in producing directories of their communities. These are generally paid for by advertising and are distributed free of charge over a wide area. It is worth pursuing this alternative at the outset as it could save your information service much time and expense (see p66).

v *What format?* This will depend to a certain extent on the number of copies to be produced and the target group. A directory aimed at the whole of a community and containing a lot of information will need to be produced as a book, rather like a telephone directory. An alternative is to publish it as a supplement to a newspaper, but this carries the danger that it will be discarded with the newspaper and not kept for reference. If you intend to produce just a small number for use by other information centres and agencies who have contact with the public, then a loose-leaf format may be more appropriate, since it allows you to send updated sheets as information changes.

vi *How is it to be distributed?* Delivered free to all households? Supplement in local newspaper? Insert in community newspaper? On request or sold at certain specified centres? Through individuals who have contact with the public or client group, eg social workers, health visitors, teachers, hoteliers, etc?

vii *Content and arrangement* It is not possible here to go into detail about the scope and arrangement of directories because these will vary depending on the nature of the directory, but the following guidelines may be of help:
  * *Scope* This should be clearly defined before you start. Decide the geographical area to be covered and the topics included. The majority of space will be taken up with entries for organizations, clubs, societies, agencies, firms, services, etc but most directories include a certain amount of 'hard'

information. This may be descriptive (profile of
area, places of interest, economic base), historical,
statistical (financial statements, population, production), legal (regulations, byelaws, rights) or
policy (development, planning).
* *Detail of entries* This will depend on who the
directory is aimed at. If you are producing it for
use by other information agencies or community
workers, then you may need to provide the full
range of information collected for your resources
file (see pp70-73) as the agency or person using the
directory will need as much information as possible
in order to assess the usefulness of an organization
to their client. For general use, it is best not to
give too much detailed information as this may
result in confusion and render the directory too
cumbersome for efficient use. The minimum
amount of information for each entry should give

```
YOUR PLACE

Young People's Information and Action Centre
2 The High Street, Middletown        Tel: 519

Contact name:      Jill Smith

Mon, Wed, Fri      10 am - 3 pm
Tues, Thurs         6 pm - 9 pm
No appointment necessary

Primarily intended for young people aged 11-18 and living within
the Middletown area.

Services provided:

information:                        all subjects

advice and practical assistance:    housing, employment, financial
                                    and welfare rights

specialist adviser:                 qualified solicitor available
                                    (Tues 6 pm - 8 pm, appointment necessary)

special services:                   representation given or arranged at
                                    housing and welfare rights tribunals
```

Figure 21 Full directory entry (from: Who knows? Guidelines
for a review of local advice and information services and how
to publicise them. *National Consumer Council, 1982, 17)*

Charities/Voluntary Organisations

Forces Help Society and Lord Roberts Workshops
Hon. Rep: D.K. Christy, 5 New Street, St. Neots, Huntingdon, Cambs. Tel: Huntingdon 74061.

Guide Dogs for the Blind
Mrs. G. Fry, 16 Hawthorn Road, Folksworth. Tel: Peterborough 241947. Meet 98 Chestnut Avenue, Dogsthorpe, 1st Tuesday of the month at 7.30pm.

Heart Foundation (British)
Peterborough Branch. Secretary: T.T.F. Harding, Beadles Residence, Town Hall, Peterborough. Tel: Peterborough 63141 or 62487.

Heartline Association
For families and friends of children with heart conditions. Local Organiser: Mrs. Plowright, 21 Lowther Gardens, Werrington, Peterborough. Tel: Peterborough 74771.

Figure 22 Short directory entries (from: Evening Telegraph Peterborough Area Local Directory)

the name of the organization, persons to contact, address or telephone number, and a brief description of the aims of the organization where this is not self-evident from the name. The two examples illustrated here (Figs 21 and 22) show a full and a short directory entry.

* *Arrangement* Again, this will depend largely on the nature of the directory. Most directories are a ranged in broad subject groups which may be further sub-divided. In each group or sub-group an alphabetical arrangement by name is preferred. A contents page at the beginning is essential so that sections can be located quickly. Also include at the beginning any information that may be required

urgently, such as emergency services. Directories are used mainly for locating specific items of information quickly, so if the arrangement is not clear and well signposted, then you will need an alphabetical index. Certainly, in a directory for use by other information agencies, there will be a need to index by the subject interests of agencies or firms as well as their names. If there is more than one entry per page, then each entry should be given a running number to which the index should refer, rather than the page.

There is some very helpful advice on preparing a directory of information and advice centres in *Who knows? Guidelines for a review of local advice and information services and how to publicise them.* National Consumer Council, 1982, gratis.

5 *Current awareness bulletins*
The need for up-to-date information is a plea that is often made by workers in many spheres of activity who do not have the time themselves to search the literature. Community workers, information and advice workers, local government officers, managers, trade union officials and shop stewards are just a few of the groups who might benefit from a regular flow of information. Current awareness bulletins are one of the best ways of supplying that information. In essence a current awareness bulletin is a duplicated listing of items of information which would be of use to a certain group or groups of workers. Such items might include:
- i *Periodical articles* Title, author, précis and source (periodical, volume number, date, page numbers of article).
- ii *New publications* Author, title, publisher, date, price, address of supplier and précis.
- iii *Other new materials* Leaflets, posters, packs, audio-visual materials, etc — give title, price (if any), address of supplier, explanatory note if necessary.
- iv *Short items of 'hard' information* New regulations or legislation, benefit rate changes, changes of address or telephone number, new personnel, new services, successful cases, etc.
- v *Press releases* Subject, précis, source.

vi *Courses* Subject, dates, venue, price, address for applications.

viii *Additions to library* Author, title, publisher, date, and filing number.

Where a publication or periodical is available locally, it is helpful to state this at the end of each item using, if necessary, for brevity, some sort of code to indicate location with a key provided at the beginning or end of the bulletin. Each item should be given a distinctive number so that requests for further information, photocopies or loan of material can be identified clearly and simply. The usual method is to use a combination of the year and a running number, eg 83/1, 83/2 etc. The most common method of arranging the entries in a current awareness bulletin is to group them under subject headings with a contents page at the beginning. Under each subject group arrange entries alphabetically if there are sufficient numbers.

Before deciding to compile your own current awareness bulletin, find out what is already produced both locally and nationally as you don't want to do work that is already being done. It may be possible, with permission, to adapt an already existing bulletin to your own local use. Seek help from other agencies with compiling and finance. The bulletin shown here (Fig 23) is produced jointly by an Advice Workers Group and the public library, with finance from the local Council for Voluntary Service. If necessary, to cover costs or postage, the bulletin can be made available on payment of a subscription. You might be able to save on postage by using other people's distribution network, eg Council for Voluntary Service, library, local government.

6 *What's on*

This kind of publication is usually very popular and much appreciated by the public, but can be very time consuming to compile and costly to print in large numbers.

* *Frequency* Usually monthly but can be more or less frequent depending on the volume of entries.
* *Sources of information* Programmes of clubs, societies, theatres, etc; posters and newspaper adverts; ringing round; grapevine or word of mouth (will need to be checked out). It is advisable to set up your own system, in addition, for gathering events information. This can

HOUSING

147/83

'Housing problems? Building
repairs, fair rents, tenancy
agreement rates. How the
Chartered Surveyors Voluntary Service can help'. Free
leaflet available from Royal
Institute of Chartered Surveyors, 12 Great George
Street, London, S.W.1.

148/83

Rent - 'Going to the Rent
Officer' by David Skinner.
Amply illustrated and
delivered in plain English, a
useful guide for tenants
wishing to go it alone.
Available from South Sheffield Inner City Community
Project, 14 Ranby Road,
Sheffield, S11 7AJ, price £2.
inc. p.&p.

149/83

'Security of tenure in the
private rented sector' by
Peter Robertson and Martin
Seaward (Association of
Housing Aid, £4.50) - manual,
written by Housing Advisers,
is intended mainly for those
giving advice to private
sector landlords and tenants.
Copies from Peter Robertson,
Brent Housing Aid Centre, 196
High Road, Willesden, NW10.
Add 95p postage & packing.

150/83

'Women and homelessness' -
report by K. Glock and others.
Useful compilation of existing
data on homeless women. Published by National Cyrenians,
available from Women and Homelessness Group, 54 Devonshire
Road, Cambridge - no price
indicated.

LEGAL

151/83

County Court fees - enforcement of a judgement - new
rates listed on form EX50B
from local County Court.

152/83

'Legal aid - financial limits
as from 1st April, 1983' - new
edition of free leaflet,
copies from address No. 3.

PERSONAL

153/83

'Gays and the law' by Paul
Crane (Pluto Press, £4.95) -
book primarily for gay men
giving thorough review of
police practice and examples
of abuse in law enforcement,
together with recommen-
dations for a gay movement
strategy to liberalise the
law. Useful advice on presenting a defence to criminal
charges.

154/83

'Personal application for probate or letters of administration' (Form PR48) - new
edition of form. Copies free
from Probate Office, Clifton
House, Broadway, Peterborough.

TRANSPORT

155/83

'Children's safety in cars' -
new leaflet describes how the
new seat belt legislation
affects children and gives
advice on carry cot re-
straints, child safety seats
and restraints and booster
cushions. Copies free from
Education Section, BSI, 2 Park
Street, London, W1A 2BS.

*Figure 23   Page from Peterborough Council for Voluntary
Service's* Advice workers news

include keeping a diary in your centre in which organizers of events can write their dates, providing a tear off slip in each month's *What's On,* or sending the major venues a sheaf of slips pre-printed with the headings of the information you require.

* *Basic information for each entry* Date, event, organizer, place, time, admission/ticket price (if any), where to obtain tickets. Write each event on a standard card or slip (see Fig 24) so that whoever prepares the list (typist or printer) can do so consistently.

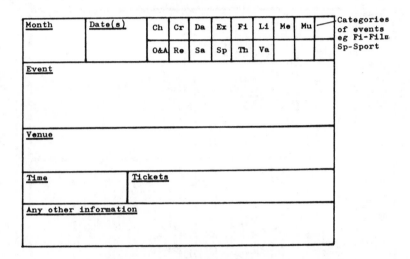

Month	Date(s)	Ch	Cr	Da	Ex	Fi	Li	Me	Mu	Categories of events eg Fi-Film Sp-Sport
		O&A	Re	Sa	Sp	Th	Va			
Event										
Venue										
Time		Tickets								
Any other information										

Figure 24 Slip for recording forthcoming events

* *Arrangement* A small number of entries can be arranged straightforwardly by date, but larger numbers are best divided initially by categories, such as theatre, dances, films, exhibitions, etc, and then by date.
* Use illustrations to add interest as an unrelieved list of dates can be very boring on the eye.

Ideally *What's on*s should be free but, if necessary, add a small cover charge to cover costs or use advertising. You may be able to interest a commercial publisher or newspaper in producing the list or get sponsorship from local firms, as in the example below (Fig 25), with your information service contributing the dates and being suitably acknowledged.
Distribute lists as widely as possible and, where you can

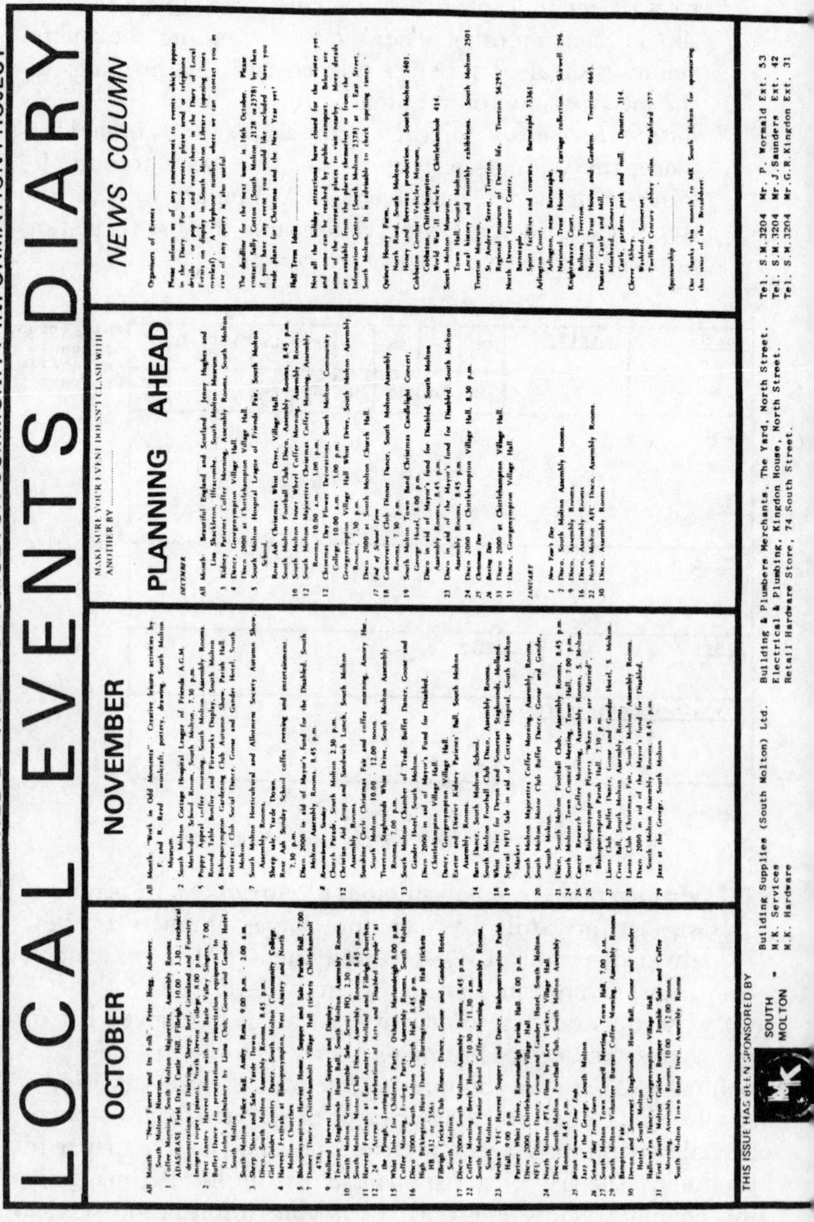

THIS BROADSHEET IS PUBLISHED BY THE SOUTH MOLTON COMMUNITY INFORMATION PROJECT

LOCAL EVENTS DIARY

OCTOBER

NOVEMBER

MAKE SURE YOUR EVENT DOESN'T CLASH WITH ANOTHER BY ....

PLANNING AHEAD

NEWS COLUMN

THIS ISSUE HAS BEEN SPONSORED BY

MK SOUTH MOLTON - Building & Plumbers Supplies (South Molton) Ltd. Building & Plumbers Merchants, The Yard, North Street. Tel. S.M.3204 Mr. P. Wormald Ext. 53

M.K. Services Electrical & Plumbing, Kingdon House, North Street. Tel. S.M.3204 Mr.J.Saunders Ext. 42

M.K. Hardware Retail Hardware Store, 74 South Street. Tel. S.M.3204 Mr.G.R.Kingdon Ext. 31

Figure 25 News from the South Molton Information Centre. *Reproduced by kind permission of Devon Library Services.*

afford it, have special dispensers made to hold a supply —
these are much appreciated by those who are willing to make
supplies available.

7 *Handbooks*
These may contain some directory-type information but
mainly the text comprises descriptive information, ie about
services, rights of individuals or groups, advice on personal
matters, courses of action, etc. Handbooks can be aimed at
one particular group of people with special needs, such as
elderly people, small businessmen, the disabled, parents of
children under five, or they may cover a range of topics within
a defined geographical area. You will probably need to get
help with writing the text from people who have knowledge
of the subject. The arrangement of the handbook will depend
to a certain extent on its subject but a simple method is to
use broad headings arranged alphabetically. A contents page
and index are essential for locating specific items of information quickly. Use illustrations to break up text and add
interest. Handbooks can be expensive to produce and you
will probably need to get help with finance. Try local authorities, area health authorities, groups who represent those
covered by the handbook, national trusts and foundations,
or local charities, like Lions, Rotary Clubs, Junior Chambers
of Commerce, etc.

8 *Other publications*
There are many other publications which an information
service might like to consider, such as accommodation lists,
halls for hire, places to visit, shopping guides, access guides
for the disabled, etc. Each one may require a different
arrangement or format, method of compiling or distribution,
but they are all just as much an important part of your
information service as face to face answering of enquiries
over a desk. The quality of an information service, for good
or bad, is often judged by the quality of its publications,
especially by those who may not have used the service before.
So make sure that your publications are accurate as possible,
easy to read and attractive to the eye.

(h) *Packs* Packs are an increasingly popular form of making
information available, especially to your people, for whom
books may be too square! They are also useful for infor-

mation centres which have limited staff input and the service
is largely of the self-help type. Packs vary from a simple
plastic bag to specially embossed or printed folders. Their
chief attraction is that they enable a number of flimsy items,
such as leaflets, information sheets, lists, small booklets,
flow-charts, forms, photocopies of periodical articles, book-
lists and address lists, on a particular subject, to be brought
together and linked, if necessary by a specially prepared text.
Packs are easily duplicated for location at outlying centres
and, well produced, can entice people to browse through
them who otherwise would not use a more conventional
book form.

Some of the disadvantages of packs are that they need to
be displayed face outwards for maximum impact, they need
to be regularly checked and updated (less easy the more they
are dispersed), and they can so easily appear to be just a rag-
bag of assorted ephemera without careful and attractive
presentation.

The following guidelines may be helpful in preparing packs:
* *Choose the topic* — this might well be (i) a subject of
  frequent enquiry, eg buying and selling a house, adop-
  tion, legal aid; (ii) a subject on which there is very little
  information in book form or what exists is not readily
  understandable to the lay person eg pensions, VAT
  registration; or (iii) a subject that meets the needs of a
  particular group eg one parent families, bankrupts.
* *Identify* suitable material and obtain in required quan-
  tities.
* *Write or compile* any linking material, lists of addresses
  and further sources of information. Get help from
  people who have special knowledge of the subject, if
  necessary.
* *Number* items and list them on a contents sheet.
* *Design* a title sheet which can be inserted into or stuck
  on the pack.

Manilla wallets for packs can be obtained at most stationers,
usually in A4 or foolscap sizes. You may be lucky and find
a stationer who stocks ready-made transparent plastic folders
but, if not, Celsur Plastics Ltd, Norfolk House, Drake
Avenue, Gresham Road, Staines, Middlesex (tel 0784 53130)
will make them to your order, the price varies according to
quantity ordered but should be in the region of 10-20p each

(1983 prices). Printed coloured plastic folders will be much more expensive and are most often used for prestige in giving out information to clients of businesses, etc and are unlikely to be within the budget of a small information service.

(i) *The media* Newspapers and local radio, in particular, can be important vehicles for getting information to the public, in addition to their usual fare of shock!, horror!, crisis! stories. Television, including regional variants, is still geared more to entertainment and major news items but the advent of cable television could present the same opportunities as local radio does now. Like most organizations in these times, both newspapers and local radio have had to trim their staffing with the result that they will now more readily accept offers of free material from outside organizations, provided it is presented to them in the right way and would be of interest to a significant part of their readership or audience. The great advantage in using the media is that your information will reach a much wider audience than it ever would by any other means of dissemination even if that means is not a very permanent one. Of course, the decision as to how that information is presented to the public will be out of your control. However, I have found that in the case of regular articles, columns or scripts, provided you have clear guidelines on what is required by the particular media in terms of length, style and contents and keep to them, the material will not be altered very much.

The kind of topics in which the media might well be interested are: (i) forthcoming events, either generally or of a particular kind (eg sports, arts, etc); (ii) information on new services or groups; (ii) important changes in legislation affecting people's lives; (iv) reviews of new publications; (v) know your rights; (vi) know your services; (vii) help for businessmen; (viii) information for young people (jobs, education, rights, recreation, etc).

Think carefully about taking part in 'live' phone-in programmes on radio if this is offered. You won't be able to bring your information service into the studio and you can lay yourself open to all kinds of trouble by giving instant advice or information over the air without being able to check its accuracy first.

There is obviously some overlap between giving out information via the media and publicising your service through the media, which is dealt with in the next chapter. Just giving out information, provided your service is credited, is a form of publicity, but I will confine myself here to just a few pointers on using the media for purely information giving:

* Contact the media — make sure they know about your information service and what it can provide.
* Find out if there is a reporter who covers the areas of interest of your service and get to know him or her.
* Regularly feed information to the media.
* Make yourself available for interview on topics of interest to your information service, even at what might be an inconvenient time for you.
* Don't be put off by one bad experience with the media — tomorrow is another day.

Further information on using the media, including recommended reading, will be found on p127.

I have concentrated in this chapter on the dissemination of information collected by an information service and available in its files. All the methods covered above can also be used to disseminate information about the service itself. This is publicity and is the subject of the next chapter.

References
1. The Graphic Communications Centre Ltd, Bernard House, Granville Road, Maidstone, Kent ME14 2BJ publish a range of instant art books including:
    Instant art. Books One and Two
    Instant borders and frames
    Instant symbols and graphics
    Instant archive art — old engravings and period art
    Instant colour art

Chapter Five

Publicity and promotion

It is simply not enough to set up an information service and expect people to come flocking to your door. There will always be some persistent souls who find their way, however much you hide your light under a bushel. Nevertheless, as a general rule, people need to be continually and effectively reminded of the existence of your service and what it can offer, since it is never possible to predict the time when they might have need of it. Therefore, you need to make publicity available through a variety of forms and outlets, according to the finances available. The following are the main methods of publicising a service which will be considered here:

* name and logo
* posters and leaflets
* displays
* the media and video
* talks
* advertising

Name and logo
Opinion tends to be divided over the necessity for an information service to have a distinctive name. I believe it is important for potential users of a service to have a name that is easily memorable and indicates something of the nature of that service. It is particularly important where the service marks a new departure for an existing organization which may not be readily associated in people's minds with the new service offered. This was born out by the experience of Lambeth Libraries who, when they set up an information service for small businesses called LINK (Lambeth Infor-

mation Network), found that many of the callers were
completely unaware that the service was part of the public
library. Some of the more successful community information
services set up by libraries in the USA, Britain and Australia
have distinctive names which feature on letter headings,
articles, and publicity of all kinds (Fig 26).

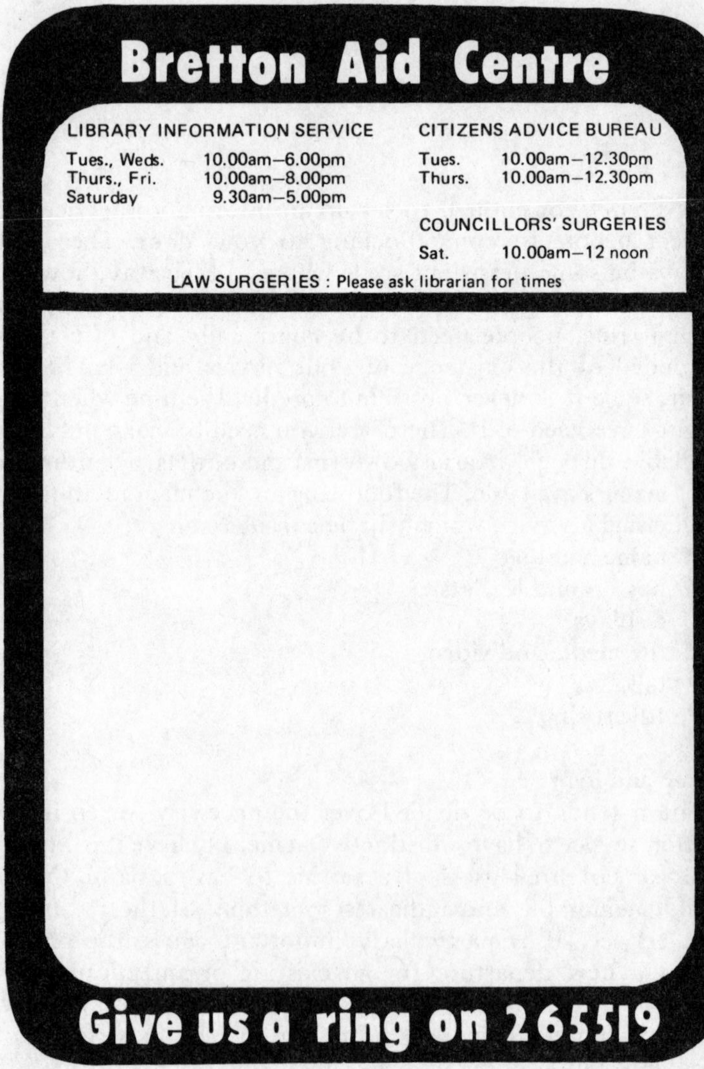

Bretton Aid Centre

LIBRARY INFORMATION SERVICE

Tues., Weds.	10.00am–6.00pm
Thurs., Fri.	10.00am–8.00pm
Saturday	9.30am–5.00pm

CITIZENS ADVICE BUREAU

Tues.	10.00am–12.30pm
Thurs.	10.00am–12.30pm

COUNCILLORS' SURGERIES

Sat.	10.00am–12 noon

LAW SURGERIES : Please ask librarian for times

Give us a ring on 265519

Figure 26 Bretton Aid Centre notepad

In addition to a distinctive name, it is helpful to have a symbol or logo which people can instantly recognize and gives the service a sense of identity.

Posters and leaflets

A simple and effective means to advertise your information service is to produce posters, handbills or leaflets for display and distribution from a wide vareity of outlets. These do not necessarily have to be sophisticated or expensive, some quite impressive results can be achieved using minimal resources with a bit of imagination. See books listed on page 125 for ideas and how to do it.

i *Posters* are an easy way to get small amounts of information across. They should only give the name of the service, address, telephone number, hours of opening and, where necessary, any explanatory words to make it clear what kind of service is offered and to whom. To be effective a poster has got to catch people's attention, so concentrate on this aspect of the design rather than getting in as many words as possible. It is more important that you create the right image of your service than to bombard the potential user with information. Using 'day glo' paper (that's the stuff with light reflecting colours) can give striking results but may not be suitable for all occasions. Try to get your posters displayed in as many places as possible: libraries, community centres, shops, clinics, surgeries, local government offices, sports centres, schools, youth clubs, anywhere that people gather in any numbers. It is best to keep the poster as small as possible, especially if you want others to display it permanently. Certainly no bigger than A3 size (298mm × 420mm) and preferably A4 (210mm × 298mm).

ii *Handbills* are usually single unfolded sheets of paper, either A4 size or, more commonly, A5 (149mm × 105mm), printed on one or both sides. A quick and simple way to produce a handbill is to use the same design as your poster reduced in size. Most printers have a process camera which can do this at a small cost or you can use a photocopier which has reduction facilities. If necessary, the other side of the handbill can be used to give more details of your service. Handbills are best suited for placing on counters, tables or any flat or sloping service for people to take, for handing out in the street or other public places, or for inserting in community and local newspapers, magazines or other organizations' mail shots.

CONSUMER PROTECTION DEPARTMENT

Enforces, consumer protection legislation, such as the Weights & Measures Act, Trade Descriptions Act, Consumer Protection Act, etc. Advises traders on their obligations under the legislation and investigates complaints from the public.

Consumer Protection Department,
St. Peter's Road,
Peterborough.
Tel: 51577

Open:
Monday — Friday   8.45 a.m. — 1.00 p.m.
                   2.00 p.m. — 5.20 p.m.
Area Controller: R. Slater

Figure 27 Part of Peterborough Information Group's leaflet

iii *Leaflets* are one of the main methods of letting people know about the service you provide. They may be similar in size to a handbill, A5, or the most popular size 1/3A4 (99mm × 210mm) and will consist of one or more folds to produce several sides of which the front should be an attractive design to encourage people to pick it up. As well as the basic information contained on the poster or handbill, a leaflet can also include more description of the kind of service provided. However, still keep words to the absolute minimum, quality rather than quantity is the watchword. The leaflet should be clear, easy to read and to the point. Use illustrations or cartoons to break up the text and give added emphasis to the words (see Fig 27). A leaflet is as much about creating an image of the service as it is about giving information. Take a leaf from commercial advertising which often says nothing or very little about the product but tries to create a right frame of mind, even an irresistible urge, towards it. You don't have to go quite that far, but the principle's the same.

The following books can be recommended for practical advice on producing posters, handbills and leaflets:
A basic guide to making posters and tickets. Salford CVS, King Street, Eccles, Manchester M30, 40.
Fry, Alan *Layout & design.* Sunderland Community Press, 420 Hylton Road, Sunderland, 1981, 45p.
Gough, John *In print.* Batsford, 1979.
'Print: hints, advice and encouragement to design and print your own publications' (Action Notes No. 19) In: *Community action* No. 62.
Writing plain English. Plain English Campaign, 78 Wiltshire Street, Salford, Lancs M7 0BD, 1980.
Zeitlyn, Jonathan *Print: how you can do it yourself.* 3rd ed. Inter-Action Inprint, 1980.

Displays
In the last chapter your attention was drawn to the usefulness of displays for getting over information to a wider audience. The same methods and outlets can also be used to promote your own service. Try to present as many aspects of your information service as possible, at the same time keeping it simple. Wording should be large and clear enough to be read at a distance and relatively brief. Displays are essentially visual, so try to get some good photographs to illustrate your service, not obviously posed ones but more candid camera style. Small photographs, however good, do not make an impact on a large display, so try to get enlargements whenever possible and affordable. Enlist the help of a friendly amateur photographer with an enlarger for blowing-up black and white photographs or, failing that, Fotopost Express Ltd, Argyle Way, Stevenage, Herts SG1 2AR do a 'Fotoposter' (up to 20in X 30in) from black and

white or colour negatives and slides for £6.95 each (1983 prices).

Another way to get your service known is to have a manned exhibition, display or stand at large shows, such as agricultural shows, trade fairs, country fairs, ideal home exhibitions, markets, leisure fairs, etc. In addition to providing a static display about your service, you might also consider running an enquiry or advice service on the spot, but be sure that you can deliver the goods, since failure will reflect badly on your service. Don't expect to get too many enquiries, however, as most people attend shows and the like to enjoy themselves and leave their problems at home. It helps to have some sort of gimmick to attract attention, like the monster puzzle shown here (Fig 28) used by Peterborough Information Group at a local agricultural show. The same year, the group also borrowed two pigs for a 'Guess the weight of the pigs' competition, with proceeds going to two local organizations for the handicapped.

Figure 28 Peterborough Information Group jigsaw at East of England Show.

If the cost of taking part in this kind of show is too prohibitive on your own, investigate the possibility of sharing with other organizations or 'renting' space in someone else's exhibition. Remember to allow for sufficient staffing to cover the hours of the show, let staff have breaks for meals, etc, and continue your usual service. You will also need to arrange transport for display boards and equipment to and after the show.

It is always difficult to assess and virtually impossible to calculate how valuable such exercises are in attracting extra custom to a service. If they do no more than bring the service before the eyes of a great number of people who probably knew nothing about it before, then it may be all worth while.

The media

Press, radio and television are important means of publicising your information service, since they offer the potential of reaching many thousands of people from all walks of life. They are also transitory media and so need to be used regularly to carry your message. It is no good thinking that an advertisement placed five years ago when your service was set up, is still going to attract users! There are basically three forms that publicity about your service could take on any media: general features about the service, news items, and advertisements or commercials.

* *Newspapers* are likely to be the most common method of publicising your service. There are four main types: the national press, local newspapers, advertising papers, and community newspapers. The latter are usually non-commercial and serve a fairly defined neighbourhood, often being delivered to every door free of charge. They are a good means of getting your service known as advertising is cheaper than their commercial counterparts and may even be free for a service that helps the community. Community newspapers are likely to be more receptive to feature articles about your service.

    Advertising newspapers are also, as a rule, delivered free to every door in their catchment area but since the total cost has to be met by advertising, the rates are usually high. Many of them used to be straight news-

papers and still carry a certain amount of news as well
as adverts but not feature lenght articles. They may not
be read as thoroughly as newspapers for which there is
a charge, since there is a tendency to regard anything
free as being of little value.

The weekly or daily local newspaper is the one with
which most people will be familiar, though it is a dying
breed. It contains a mixture of news, features and advertising and, next to the community newspaper, will be
the most accessible. Some actually have a column for
community service adverts which can be placed free or
at a cheaper rate. Local newspapers are often receptive
to feature articles either written by their own staff or,
more often nowadays, by organizations themselves.
Write to the editor, tell him or her about your service
and ask if they would welcome an article. If so, you will
need to know how many words and whether there is a
deadline by which the article must be in. With this kind
of article, it is a common practice for newspapers to
hold on to it until there is a slack news day.

But what sells newspapers more than anything else
is news which, in journalistic terms, is some happening
or event that creates either conflict, hardship and danger
to the community or a scandal; features something
unusual, or displays individualism. As well as news-
worthiness, newspapers also look for that magic ingredi-
ent 'human interest'. Telling them about what you do
every day of the week doesn't constitute news, however
worthy it may be. Unusual requests or happenings are,
even when they are not directly related to the service
you are giving, as the photograph shown here (Fig
29) which appeared in the local press as a result
of a pet mouse being found in a reference library.
The schoolboy owner later came back to claim his
missing property!

The customary way to notify the media about news
concerning an organization or service is to issue a press
release. There are some simple guidelines for presenting
and writing press releases which will help to bring
your news to the attention of an editor and prevent
it from being instantly consigned to the waste paper
basket.

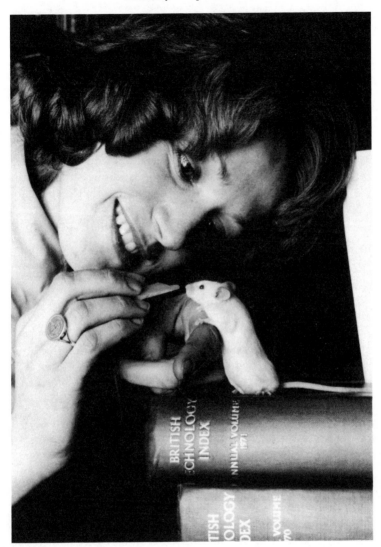

Figure 29 Mousekeeping at Peterborough Reference Library

Press releases
Presentation:
(a) Use A4 size headed paper, ideally specially designed with the name of your service, logo and the words 'Press Release' figuring prominently.

(b) Put a date at the top.
(c) Don't write it in longhand — type it, using double-spacing and provide generous margins so that the subeditor of the newspaper can re-write and add instructions for the printer.
(d) Type on one side of the paper and only go on to a second sheet if absolutely necessary, in which case put the word 'more' or mf (more follows) prominently at the bottom of the first sheet.
(e) Provide a simple heading at the top of the press release to indicate what it is about. It does not have to be a 'catchy' heading, that's the sub-editor's job.
(f) At the end of the press release put 'Ends' separately from the final sentence.
(g) Always put a name and telephone number of a person or persons from whom further information can be obtained.
(h) Staple more than one sheet together at top.

Writing:
(a) Every press release should answer the five w's: *What* is happening? *Who* is doing it? *Where* is it happening? *When* is it happening? *Why* is it happening? The answers to the first four w's should be contained in the first sentence or two, though not necessarily in the order given.
(b) The first two sentences are crucial and should contain the bare bones of your news story, so that a busy editor can see at a glance what the release is about. You can elaborate later. This is the way, you will notice, that most news stories are written. It allows the editor to cut off paragraphs from the end of a story to fit it into the final page layout without losing the gist of the item.
(c) Keep sentences short.
(d) Use active rather than passive voice. *Don't* say 'A leaflet has been issued today by Exville Information & Advice Centre . . .' *Do* say 'Exville Information & Advice has launched today a leaflet on housing rights . . .'

(e) Never use jargon and spell out acronyms the first time they are used in the press release.

(f) Use quotes where possible — journalists love these because it sounds as though they have actually been out and interviewed someone.

Specimen press release:

EXVILLE INFORMATION & ADVICE CENTRE,
10, High Street,
Exville
EX1 2AB
Tel. 67890

PRESS RELEASE   31st May 1983

HOUSING RIGHTS LEAFLET HELPS TENANTS

Exville Information & Advice Centre has launched today a leaflet* on housing rights for tenants living in private rented accommodation. It follows a sharp rise in enquiries to the Centre concerning harassment by landlords, lack of repairs and increased rents. The leaflet sets out in simple language what action tenants can take, including the withholding of rent, prosecution for trespass, and making a complaint to the Rent Officer.

Joe Bloggs, Chairman of Exville Tenants' Association, says 'I welcome this leaflet as it will bring to the attention of tenants that they do not have to put up with damp walls, leaking roofs and peeling paintwork or landlords who are out to make a fast buck.'

The leaflet is available free of charge from Exville Information & Advice Centre and all libraries and community centres in the town.

ENDS

Further information contact:
Doris Smith Tel. Exville 12345 (home), 67890 (work)
*copy attached.

It is highly unlikely that a local information service will need to use the national press to publicise its services, although there may be occasions, when a service has done or is planning something very unusual, controversial or spectacular, that it might be worthwhile to interest the national press, especially if the event would be of interest to other information services. However, for information services with a national clientele, the national press may well be an appropriate outlet for their news. The usual approach will be a press release of the type indicated above. In cases it may be possible to identify a certain columnist who takes an interest in community services and make a direct approach to interest him or her in a feature article on your service. You should also consider sending your press releases to The Press Association, Fleet Street, London EC4. This is a national press agency and, if you can get them to take up your news item, it will be fed to every important newsroom in the country. But the news will need to be pretty important or dramatic.

Magazines, specialist journals and current awareness bulletins are other possible outlets for publicising a nationally based information service. You should by now be aware of the periodicals which cover the areas of work relating to your service but, if you need further titles, both *Willings press guide* and the *Newspaper press directory* contain lists of periodicals arranged under subject headings. One or both of these will be found at most medium to large public libraries.

* *Radio* The expansion of both the BBC and IBA local radio networks in recent years has meant that most major urban areas of the country and much of the rural hinterland is served by at least one and sometimes more radio stations. Most of these stations are readily accessible to community organizations and services, probably more so than local newspapers, and will usually be pleased to broadcast announcements/events free of charge. Keep details for such announcements as brief as possible, the essentials being event, date, time, place, name of person to contact and telephone number. Send details to the radio station well in advance and, if they feel that the event is of general public interest, you may be asked to come into the studio for interview or be interviewed over the telephone. If you possibly can, it is better to go to the studio for interviews since the sound quality will be infinitely better and there is a tendency to be indiscreet over the telephone. It will also enable you to make contact with

the station staff and familiarize yourself with the studio.

You may be able to interest the radio station in doing a feature about your service and, if you're lucky, they may even let you decide the format and questions. In which case, you will need to know how long the programme is to last and whether there are to be any breaks for commercials or records. As a general rule, radio producers do not like too much unrelieved talking as listeners soon lose concentration. About four to four and a half minutes is the maximum, that's equivalent to roughly two pages of A4 double-line typing.

Other tips on being interviewed are:

(a) Try to find out in advance of an interview what questions you are going to be asked or what topics are going to be covered.

(b) Jot down on one side of a card or a piece of paper the important points you want to make, names, figures, etc which are easily forgotton when you are on air.

(c) Find out the interviewer's first name and use it when answering questions: 'I'm glad you asked that, Bob, we feel that not enough people are aware . . .'. It sounds less of a confrontation, oral examination or third degree interrogation.

(d) Never get annoyed or flustered if an interviewer is aggressive; by remaining calm and friendly you will only show up his or her bad manners and gain the listeners' sympathy.

(e) Never be afraid to say 'I don't know' to a question; it is far better than inventing wrong information or blustering and you can always use the opportunity to answer a question that hasn't been asked: 'I don't know what the answer to that is, Rita, but there is evidence of tenants being harassed by . . .'.

(f) Will yourself to speak slowly because there is a natural tendency to talk much too fast on radio. However, avoid embarrassing pauses whenever possible.

(g) If the programme is pre-recorded, don't be afraid to say 'Can we do that again' when you are making a bad reply; it can always be edited out.

(h) Avoid sarcasm — the listener cannot see your face and so will not know whether you are joking or not.

(i) Put a smile in your voice.

(j) Never rustle papers during or at the end of an interview, it soulds like a simulated storm at the receiving end.

With the financial resources and the expertise, you could have a go at producing an advertisement slot for broadcasting on commercial radio stations. You will, however, be competing with firms and businesses for the available time and the prime periods throughout the day when most people tune in. I don't know if my local radio station is typical or not but their charges for producing a commercial at 1983 prices start at £40 and increase depending on the length, number of voices used, music, sound effects, etc. Broadcasting rates vary from £3.25 for a twenty second spot on weekday and Sunday evenings after 6pm to £54 for the same time between 6am and 9am Monday-Friday, 9am-10 noon Saturday and Sunday. Your local radio station will be able to advise you on the best time to reach the particular clientele served by your information service. Producing a commercial is a skilled exercise and it is worth getting expert help from an advertising agency or the local radio station itself.

For further information on using local radio see:
Local radio kit. Community Projects Volunteers/National Extension College, 1982.
Brand, John *Hello, good evening and welcome.* Shaw & Son, 1982 — also covers television interviews.
See also further information at end of next section.

* *Television* Access to television for local or nationally-based information services is limited but not impossible. It is unlikely that a service would be able to afford the vast sums of money necessary to produce their own programme or commercial and buy air time, but there are now a number of programmes on all channels which give access to community groups. Obviously, the pro-

ducers of such programmes must get more than enough requests for inclusion but you may be lucky and catch their interest especially if your service is offering something different or innovative. A list of both radio and television programmes covering social action, social welfare and community information services can be found in the bi-annual *Directory of social action programmes* produced by the Media Project (address below).

In addition to those social action programmes, many of the commercial television stations offer the facility of Public Service Announcements. These enable local voluntary, statutory and community organizations the opportunity to 'advertise' in short slots between programmes throughout the week. Organizations can appeal for volunteers, recruit new members to self-help groups, offer services and advice to the public, or increase awareness of an interest in the work of the organization. There is no charge for the announcements and usually help is given with producing the slot. Write to your local IBA television company to find out if they run such a scheme. Addresses can be found in *Television and radio: the IBA guide* (Independent Television Publications Ltd, annual) which will be found in most public libraries. Channel 4 are also doing some interesting community access programmes as Public Service Announcements. Contact them at Channel 4 Television, 60 Charlotte Street, London W1p 2AX. They produce a useful magazine which gives details of these programmes called *See 4*. You can be put on the mailing list by writing to Derek Jones, Educational Liaison Officer, at the same address.

Further information on television and radio can be obtained from: Media Project, The Volunteer Centre, 29 Lower Kings Road, Berkhamsted, Herts HP4 2AB. This project collects and disseminates information on initiatives in the general area of community involvement through TV and radio. They produce a quarterly bulletin called *Media Project news*, the *Directory of social action programmes* mentioned above and a series of 'Media Case Studies'.

There is a useful article entitled 'Broadcasting and your organisation' in *NCVO information service* No 95

July 1983 pp11-17. National Council for Voluntary Organisations, 26 Bedford Square, London WC1B 3HU.

* *Video* is being increasingly used by community organizations to promote their services, in staff training or to draw attention to a social or local problem. Video equipment is relatively easy to handle and portable, videocassettes are cheap and can be used over and over again, and playback can take place in any room which has an ordinary television set. Video equipment is quite expensive but it can often be loaned or hired from schools, colleges, adult evening institutes, video workshops, community art centres or some video shops. If you are interested in using video to promote your service the following books may be of help:
   Basic video. CATS, Dept, 42 Theobalds Road, London WC1, £2.25.
   Basic video in community work. Inter-Action Inprint, 1975, £0.75.
   Video. Grapevine, BBC TV, London W12 8QT – free, send sae.
   Wade, Graham *Street video.* Blackthorn Press, 74 Highcross Street, Leicester LE1 4NW, 1981, £2.10 – describes activities of five video groups. Removes some of the mystique from video.

The following books will give you a good introduction to the media in general:
How to handle the media: a guide for trade unionists. TUC Publications, 1979, 60p.
Dealing with the media. Directory of Social Change, 1978.
MacShane, Denis *Using the media.* Pluto Press, 1979.

Talks
An effective and inexpensive way to publicize your information service is by giving talks to the multifarious groups in the community who are constantly on the look out for speakers. Although the membership of such groups may be small in numbers, it is an opportunity not only to tell people about the service you offer but also, in discussion and questions afterwards, to get feedback from them on their needs and the effectiveness of your service. Never underestimate the power

of the grapevine, you may be only talking to a handful of old dears, but they have the ability to pass the word on to a much wider circle.

Keep talks as brief as possible, use simple language and, where suitable, visual aids. A touch of humour, in the right place and taste, helps to get the audience on your side. Give-aways, in the form of leaflets, booklets, information sheets, etc are often much appreciated. If possible, invite groups to visit your premises where information resources and equipment can be demonstrated — this never fails to impress.

Advertising

It is unlikely that many information services will be able to afford this type of publicity. Poster sites are not cheap and, to be effective, the publicity will need to be professionally done. Obviously, the best sites are where a lot of people gather or pass by, such as railway stations, buses, bus stops and stations, shopping malls, and town centres. If your service is part of a larger organization like a local government authority, then they may own poster sites of their own or run the transport system. So it may, in those cases, be possible to advertise your service in a prominent site. You could always try writing to advertising agencies or owners of poster sites to see if they would donate space to your service for the public good — you never know, your plea might fall on a sympathetic ear.

At the end of the day, whatever method of publicity you use or however much or little you spend, the best publicity is a service that is successful in meeting the needs of its clientele, for news will spread by word of mouth from satisfied users. The way to ensure that your service is achieving all that it set out to do or to find out if it ought to be doing more, is to keep it under continual review. In the next chapter we shall be looking at various methods of doing this.

Further reading

Publicity information guide. Islington Bus Company, Palmer Place, London N7 8DA, 1981, 40p.
Sladen, C *Getting across: a publicity primer for voluntary organisations.* Bedford Square Press, 1973.

'Communicating for your organisation; a practical guide.' Parts One and Two. In *NCVO information service.* Nos 85, Sept. 1982 and 86, Oct. 1982 pp11-14, 17-21.

Lewis, Dilys R *How to get the message over.* National Federation of Community Associations, 1979, £1.50.

Chapter Six

How to maintain an effective service

An information service needs to be flexible in order to respond to the changing needs of the community it serves. Therefore, the final element, and a very important one, in planning a service is to provide a means of continually monitoring its effectiveness. You need to know whether the right information is being collected and the right clientele reached, where, if any, there are gaps in provision, and how effective is the publicity for your service. There are several ways of monitoring a service, each with varying degrees of complexity. The method or methods you choose will depend on the amount of staff time and resources you have available. They are:
* statistics
* feedback
* surveys
* research

Statistics
There are very few people who would claim to like keeping statistics. At best, they are looked on as an irksome necessity only tolerable when kept as unobtrusive as possible. Staff running a busy information service will seldom have time to keep detailed records of enquiries, so try to restrict them to the absolute minimum.

The barest minimum is simply to record the number of persons using the centre by noting it down on a sheet of paper, using the time-honoured 'five barred gate' method (卌) or a number tally machine or 'clicker' (Fig 30). This will only tell the numbers of people who darkened your doorstep, they might have only been browsing or sheltering from the rain, so an alternative is to record the number of people making an enquiry, by using the same methods as above. However, you will still not know either what subjects they enquired about, whether you were successful in finding the information, or how long it took.

Figure 30 Rexel hand tally machine

You can go some way towards collecting more detail and yet not create very much more work by drawing up or pre-printing record sheets with headings of certain categories of enquiries. These may be related to subject or length of time or both (Fig 31). Some centres, instead of using sheets, have a bank of 'clickers', but this is only practicable if you have a small number of categories, say no more than six, otherwise it becomes too complicated to remember which 'clicker' is which.

All the above methods only give a broad indication of the numbers of enquiries and do not reveal any detail about their nature or the degree of success in answering them. The latter aspect might be catered for by asking staff to record details of unsuccessful enquiries only, so that they can be analysed in order to detect any weaknesses in the information base that can be rectified or sources that have been overlooked.

A more detailed recording system found mainly in advice and counselling centres, is the day book. In effect, this is a large diary in which details of each enquiry are recorded each day, giving the name of client, address, date and nature of enquiry, action taken, further action being pursued, etc. A day book has the advantage of being easy to use and allows other information and advice workers to check on the details of an enquiry if the person calls back on another occasion. It is not so convenient for extracting statistics and when you need to refer back to an enquiry, the chronological arrangement is not helpful. People can be notoriously vague about dates. A more satisfactory method is to enter the details on cards or pre-printed enquiry forms, one for each client. These

DATE:			
	Under 5 mins.	5 – 15 mins.	Over 15 mins.
Commercial	꒰꒱꒰꒱꒰꒱ ꒱꒱	꒱꒱꒱	꒱
Housing	꒱꒱		
Tourist	꒰꒱꒰꒱꒰꒱ ꒰꒱꒰꒱꒰꒱ ꒱	꒱	

Figure 31 Enquiry record sheet — by broad categories

can then be filed by the client's name, so that it is easy to refer back if some time has elapsed between visits.

The system of pre-printed enquiry forms is fairly common in information centres but is rarely used for all enquiries, usually only those that take some time or require further search after the enquirer has left the centre. The kind of information that you may want to collect about each enquiry can include the following:

* Client: name, address, telephone number (if needed for follow-up), sex and age range.
* Enquiry — simple précis of subject.
* Sources used or tried in answering the enquiry — useful if search is continued over a length of time so that work is not duplicated.
* How enquiry was received — walk-in, telephone, telex, post.

* Time — will indicate spread of enquiries throughout the day.
* How client heard of service — may help to measure success of publicity.
* Client's area of residence (if address not taken) — will show from which areas most use comes and those not being reached.

Forms have the advantage that they can be easily stored for future reference and abstracting of statistics. With a subject heading or classification number added, they can become a subject file to be referred to when information on the same subject or statistics are required. In a very busy information centre, however, it is unlikely that staff will have time to fill in a form with this amount of detail for each enquiry, so you may need to consider a combination of (a) forms for lengthier enquiries and those needing to be followed up, and (b) a tally system under broad categories for quick enquiries.

The record sheet shown here (Fig 32) is a kind of compromise hybrid that was used for recording enquiries in a public library community information centre shared with other agencies on a sessional basis. Each agency had its own pad of forms which were self-carbonated to produce an additional copy for the librarian to extract statistics.

Feedback
Statistics can tell you how many people used your information service, how many enquiries they made, when and on what subjects but they will not reveal whether users are satisfied with the service or not or why others do not use your service. To get some idea of the impact your service is making on its community, you need to have a means of getting feedback from that community.

Two ways of doing this have already been referred to elsewhere in this book. In Chapter Two, one of the functions of the management committee of an information service was identified as to 'monitor use and recommend changes'. If, as suggested, this committee includes representatives of the community, then their comments will be very important in assessing how well the service is doing. Then in Chapter Five, it was suggested that a spin-off from publicizing a service by means of talks to community groups was that it also gave

BRETTON AID

AGENCY

DATE	QUESTION POSED			BRIEF DESCRIPTION OF INQUIRY	SOURCE USED TO ANSWER				REFERRAL TO							OTHER ACTION				QUESTIONNER					LENGTH OF TIME SPENT
	In person	Phone	Mail		Library Collection	Pamphlet	Community File	Central Library	C.P.	C.A.B.	C.H.C.	Careers	Other	Agency	Please Name	Help with form	Telephone Inquiry	Make Appointment	Write Letter	Adult *	Young Person *	Bretton Resident	First Visit	Call-back	

* PLEASE INDICATE M./F.

Figure 32 Bretton Aid Centre enquiry record sheet

an opportunity for the speaker to ask for reactions to the service and discover any needs not being met.

There is a practice, associated mainly with Information and Referral Centres in the United States, called 'follow-up' which is used to check on user satisfaction with the service or services to which they have been referred. At the time of the enquiry, details of the client's name and telephone number, the query and the service(s) to which referred are noted down. Then, at a later date, the client is rung back to find out if the information given was satisfactory or whether further help is required. Any adverse comments about the I & R centre are taken note of so that improvements can be made, comments about other services are noted down on the back of the appropriate card for that service in the Resources File. In this way, clients are encouraged to feel that they are a part of the information service and can contribute to the continual evaluation of its information files. However, follow-up is a time-consuming and costly exercise which may well be beyond the means of most information services except on an occasional and very selective basis.

You may be able to get some useful feedback by consulting other information and advice services or community leaders in your area. They may have had comments made to them about your service and be prepared to divulge them with frankness.

Surveys

A more formal and systematic way to obtain feedback is to conduct a user survey or a general survey of your community. You do not have to be an experienced researcher to carry out a survey provided you exercise a degree of commonsense and care in drafting or asking questions. Some elementary points to look out for in conducting a survey were discussed in Chapter One (p13) and are worth referring to again here.

Before you conduct a survey, you must have a clear idea of what you want to find out and the use to which that information is going to be put. You may only want to gather information about the existing clientele of your service, in which case a user survey is called for. On the other hand, it may be important to find out what impact your service is making on the community as a whole, therefore the scope of the survey needs to be wider and to be conducted outside the information centre.

There are basically two methods of conducting a survey, one is by questionnaire and the other by interview. A questionnaire survey of users is the easiest to carry out as, once the form has been drafted and printed, there is little staff involvement until the analysis stage. Questionnaires can either be left on the counter for clients to take or they can be handed to clients when an enquiry is made. Points to look out for are:

* Number forms so that you know how many have been issued and can calculate the percentage returned.
* Make sure there is an address for returning the form and a closing date — you do not necessarily have to keep to the closing date but it helps to encourage people to return them.
* Have an open question on the form to invite any other comments about the service — this often evokes the best replies.
* Arrange a system for return of forms that has a degree of anonymity (eg a posting box in the centre).

With this kind of survey, it is usual to find that responses tend to be biased towards the favourable, so you will have to allow for this when interpreting results.

The other method of surveying users is by interview. This has the advantages that it is possible for the interviewer to probe for greater depth in responses, to record qualified replies to questions rather than a straight yes/no response, and the interviewee can ask for clarification of any questions they are not sure of. A disadvantage of this method, of course, is that the more non-standardized the replies, the more difficult they are to analyse and represent statistically. You will need space in your information centre to conduct interviews and staff time, though it may be possible to enlist outside help with this in the shape of volunteers or students on placement. It is unlikely that you will be able to interview every user, so an agreed proportion must be worked out, say every other one or every tenth. Whatever the proportion, you will probably need two interviewers as it is not possible for one person to interview and keep an eye on the numbers using the service in order to catch the next one. With more than one interviewer it becomes necessary to ensure that questions are posed in the same way especially when there is a need to prompt interviewees and that means some form of training or briefing beforehand. The remarks above about allowing for favourable bias in interpreting replies also apply here, possibly to an even greater extent, since clients are unlikely to be outwardly critical of a service when being interviewed on its premises.

A survey of the wider community needs to be drafted even more carefully. Where possible try to disguise the purpose of the survey and avoid asking leading questions ('Don't you think it is a good idea to . . .') as these may colour responses. It is unlikely that with both questionnaires or interviews you will be aiming for total coverage of the community, so decide on a representative sample. There are several possible ways of distributing questionnaires, the least satisfactory being to leave copies in public buildings (community centres, libraries, council offices, shops, clinics, etc) for people to take. This is a bit hit or miss and may not result in a representative sample. A better alternative is to deliver by hand to every tenth house (or whatever proportion you have decided) using your own staff or volunteers. There may, however, be a simpler way of distributing by, for example, inserting copies in a proportion of community newspapers (where they exist) that are delivered to each household. You might investigate the possibility of printing the survey as part of the community newspaper. Where you can afford it, include a stamped addressed envelope for reply, otherwise arrange for them to be left at suitable locations in the community.

Below is an example of a survey questionnaire aimed at finding out the use made of a library community information centre. It was drafted by students at Leeds Polytechnic School of Librarianship under the direction of Judith Bowen (Fig 33).

Interviewing of the wider community to determine use is unlikely to be a practical proposition for an information centre to conduct on its own. It is more likely to be used where an outside organization is conducting a research project on your service.

Research
Surveys are one form of research of which there are a number of other types — operational research, action research, experimental research — most of which require a certain

5. HAVE YOU USED ANY OF THESE SERVICES IN PETERBOROUGH, IN THE LAST 6 MONTHS?

CITIZENS ADVICE BUREAU	
JOB CENTRE	
CONSUMER ADVICE SHOP	
TOWN HALL INFORMATION DESK	

ANY OTHER, PLEASE STATE

----

6. DO YOU USE THE CRESSET?

YES	GO TO Q7
NO	GO TO Q8

7. FOR WHAT REASON?

SHOPPING	
SPORT	
TO GO TO A DAY CENTRE	
OTHER LEISURE ACTIVITIES	

8. DO YOU USE ANY OTHER COMMUNITY CENTRE IN BRETTON?

YES	
NO	

IF SO, WHICH ONE?_____

9. WHAT OTHER ACTIVITIES SHOULD THE LIBRARY PROMOTE, AS WELL AS LENDING BOOKS AND GIVING INFORMATION.

TALKS	
EXHIBITIONS	
LEAFLETS TO TAKE AWAY	
LOANS OF POSTERS & SLIDES	
OTHER AGENCIES GIVING ADVICE IN THE LIBRARY	

THANK YOU FOR YOUR HELP.

Figure 33 Part of Library Survey conducted in Bretton Township, Peterborough by the Public Libraries Research Unit of Leeds Polytechnic School of Librarianship

amount of expertise and, therefore, will need to be conducted by an outside agency, eg the British Library, a library school, or a university department. Interest in your information service as a subject of research will depend on whether it has innovative features or the aspect to be investigated is symptomatic of other information centres and thus the research findings would have a wide applicability. For a more detailed discussion of research objectives and techniques, there is an excellent basic guide by Nick Moore called *How to do research* (Library Association, 1983).

Continuous evaluation using one or several of the techniques outlined above is essential in order to keep the service relevant to its community. By indicating strengths and weaknesses, areas of unmet need and duplication of services, it can point the way to future development of the information service. An information service needs to be a growing organism because communities do not stand still but are constantly changing, some more rapidly than others. At the beginning of this book, I stressed the need to involve the community in the planning of your information service and that is the same message at the end. An information service exists to serve its community and, therefore, the community needs to be involved at all stages. There is no guarantee, in these hard times, that your service will survive, but it stands a much better chance of succeeding and developing if it can be shown that it is respected and valued by the community and is performing a worthwhile function.

Appendix One

Model job specification for the organizer of an information service

Numbers in brackets refer to notes at the end of the specification.

Function: To provide (1) with (2) to enable them to (3). This is to be achieved through the organization of (4) designed to meet the needs of the community.

Responsibility: The organizer is responsible to (5).

Specific duties and responsibilities
1 Staff
  The organizer is responsible for
  — the recruitment and selection of suitable paid or voluntary staff to operate the service;
  — ensuring that all staff receive initial and ongoing training;
  — assessing the performance of all staff and, where necessary, recommending appropriate action to (5);
  — arranging effective communication with staff through regular meetings, staff bulletins, etc.
  — providing advice and support to all staff.

2 Administration
  The organizer is responsible for
  — establishing and maintaining an up-to-date and accurate information system to meet the needs of users of the service;
  — keeping adequate records relating to the use of the service;
  — handling correspondence;

- maintaining an adequate supply of stationery and other items;
- keeping financial records relating to the sale of items by the service and the disbursement of petty cash;
- dealing with complaints against the service;
- the security of the premises.

3 Liaison and public relations
The organizer is responsible for
- developing links with local, regional and national agencies and individuals whose work or knowledge might be of benefit to the service;
- representing the service on any appropriate bodies, committees, etc;
- publicising and promoting the service through all appropriate channels;
- drawing attention to local issues or shortcomings arising out of the work of the service;
- preparing an Annual Report.

4 Finance
The organizer, with (6), is responsible for the preparation of estimates, applications for grants and the budget.

5 Development
The organizer is responsible, with the help of (5), for
- the continual monitoring of the use made of the service and for recommending any alterations to improve the service or meet changing needs;
- the development of additional services within the centre considered necessary to meet the needs of users or potential users;
- the development of any external sessions or extensions of the service deemed to be necessary.

Notes
(1) Statement of clientele, eg the general public, members of a particular organization, residents on a certain estate, etc.
(2) Statement about the kind of service to be offered, eg information, advice, support, etc.
(3) Statement of the purpose for which the service is being provided, eg to enable people to obtain their rights, to

improve decision making, to help solve everyday problems, etc.

(4) Statement of type of organization, eg information service, support unit, current awareness service, etc.

(5) Statement of body or person ultimately responsible for the service to whom the organizer reports eg management committee, librarian, administrative officer, etc.

(6) Statement of any body or person responsible for the financial control of the service, eg treasurer, librarian, finance officer, finance sub-committee, etc.

This job specification is based on that drawn up by the National Association of Citizens Advice Bureaux for Bureau Organizer, with deletions, amendments and additions of my own in order to make it more generally applicable. Not all the responsibilities listed above will be appropriate to every type of service, so you will need to select from or add to this model in the light of your own circumstances.

Appendix Two

**List of umbrella organizations
covering information and advice services**

Advice and information services in general
Advice Services Alliance, c/o 18 Queen Anne's Gate, London
WC1B 3HU (tel. 01-222 9501).
Community Information Project, c/o Bethnal Green Library,
Cambridge Heath Road, London E2 (tel 01-981 6114).

Citizens advice bureaux
National Association of Citizens' Advice Bureaux (NACAB),
110 Drury Lane, London WC2B 5SW (tel 01-836 9231).
Northern Ireland Association of Citizens' Advice Bureaux
(NIACAB), 2 Annadale Avenue, Belfast BT7 3JH (tel 0232-
640011/3).
Scottish Association of Citizens' Advice Bureaux (SACAB),
82 Nicolson Street, Edinburgh EH8 9EW (tel 031-667
0156).

Community organizations and workers
Association of Community Workers (ACW), 22 Colombo
Street, London SE1 8DP (tel 01-633 0628).
National Council for Voluntary Organisations (NCVO),
26 Bedford Square, London WC1B 3HU (tel 01-636 4066).
National Federation of Community Organizations (NFCO),
10 Bayley Street, London WC1B 3HB (tel 01-636 1295/6).
Northern Ireland Council of Social Service (NICSS), 2
Annadale Avenue, Belfast BT7 3JH (tel 0232-640011/3).
Scottish Council of Social Service (SCSS), 18-19 Claremont
Crescent, Edinburgh EH7 4QD (tel 031-556 3882).

Consumer advice centres
Consumers Association, 14 Buckingham Street, London WC2N 6DS (tel 01-839 1222).
Institute of Consumer Advisers, 24 Aubrey Road, London E17 (tel 01-558 0033).

Disablement information and advice lines
Dial UK, Dial House, 117 High Street, Clay Cross, Derbyshire (tel 0246-864498).

Educational guidance services
Advisory Council for Adult and Continuing Education (ACACE), 19B De Montfort Street, Leicester LE1 7GE (tel 0533-542770).
National Association of Educational Guidance Services, Chairman: Jonathan Brown, LEASA, Room 10, 2 Ellison Place, Newcastle-on-Tyne NE1 6EU (tel 0632-841611/ 0632-362005).

Elderly information and advice services
Age Concern England, Bernard Sunley House, 60 Pitcairn Road, Mitcham, Surrey CR4 3LL (tel 01-640 5431).

Housing advice centres
Association of Housing Aid, c/o 36 Yewfield Road, London NW10 (tel 01-451 0231).
Shelter National Housing Aid Trust, 157 Waterloo Road, London SE1 8XF (tel 01-633 9377)

Independent/Neighbourhood advice centres
Federation of Independent Advice Centres, c/o Sheffield Advice Centres Group, 124 Devonshire Street, Sheffield 3 (tel 0742-754634).

Legal advice and law centres
Law Centres Federation, 164 North Gower Street, London NW1 2ND (tel 01-387 8570).
Legal Action Group (LAG), 28a Highgate Road, London NW5 1NS (tel 01-485 1189/01-267 0048).

Race relations
Commission for Racial Equality, Elliot House, 10-12 Allington Street, London SW1E 5EH (tel 01-828 7022).

Settlements and social action centres
British Association of Settlements and Social Action Centres (BASSAC), 7 Exton Street, London SE1 8UE (tel 01-261 1919).

Tourist information centres
English Tourist Board, 4 Grosvenor Gardens, London SW1W 0DU (tel 01-730 3400).
Northern Ireland Tourist Board, River House, 48 High Street, Belfast BT1 2DS (tel 0232-231221).
Scottish Tourist Board, 23 Ravelston Terrace, Edinburgh EH4 3EU (tel 031-332 2433).
Wales Tourist Board, Brunel House, 2 Fitzalan Road, Cardiff CF2 1UY (tel 0222-499909).

Trade union and community resource centres
Network of Labour and Community Research and Resource Centres, c/o 118 Workshop, 118 Mansfield Road, Nottingham (tel 0602 582369).

Youth counselling, advice and information centres
National Association of Young People's Counselling and Advisory Services (NAYPCAS), 17-23 Albion Street, Leicester LE1 6GD (tel 0533-554775).

Reading list

Advice and information services. Age Concern England, 1979, £1.00.

Ainley, Patricia *Basics of community information.* 2 vols. Association of Assistant Librarians, South East Division, 1980,

Kempson, Elaine *On the road: a guide to setting up and running a mobile advice centre.* Community Information Project, 1981, £2.95.

Taylor, Marilyn *Resource Centres for community groups.* Community Projects Foundation, 1983, £2.60.

Smith, Mark *Organise! A guide to practical politics for youth and community groups.* National Association of Youth Clubs Publications, 1981, £1.75.

Thorne, Kaye *Community resource centres.* Rev. ed. Bristol Settlement Community Education Centre, The Flat, 43 Ducie Road, Barton Hill, Bristol BS5 0AX, 1983, £3.25.

Telephone advice services. Community Information Project, 1981, 50p.

Working on wheels: an information pack for people interested in the use of mobile community resources. National Playbus Association, 1982, £5.50.

Index

Advertising 137
Advocacy 26
Advice 26
Alphabetization 80

Bookshelves 43-4
British Library Research &
    Development Department
    34

Card files 74-6
    equipment 39-42
Classification 90-2
Clubs and societies 69-72
Community action 27
Community education 27
Community profiles 17-19
Co-operation 21-3
Counselling 27
Current awareness bulletins
    112-13

Deposit files and collections
    102-3
Desks 37-8
Development Commission 32
Directories
    compiling 108-12
    local 66
    national 20, 66
Display boards 46-7
Displays
    publicity for information
        service 125-7
    transmission of information
        98-102

Edge-punched cards 75-6
Extension of information
    services 21

Feedback 143-4
Filing cabinets 43

Filing systems 76-90
    alphabetization 80
    'housekeeping' 81
    updating 81-4
Finance 29-35
Free material
    ordering 89
Furniture and equipment 37-
    49

'Gate-keepers' 10-11
Government grants for
    information
    services 31-3
Grants
    central government 31-3
    local government 31
    trusts 33-4
    Urban Aid 31-2

Handbills 123-4
Handbooks 117

Industry
    financial support for infor-
        mation services 34
Information
    collecting 65-73, 81-9
    storing 73-6, 84, 89-90
    types of 64-5
Information and advice services
    collection of information on
        19
    national directories 20
Information giving 26
Insurance 59-61
Interviewing 93-5

Job specification 149-51
Joint collection of information
    22